About Kilkenny

About Kilkenny

A guide to Kilkenny City and County

Mosaic of Kilkenny's two saints. On the left, St Kieran, Kilkenny's patron Saint. On the right, St Canice, after whose church, which he holds in his hands, Kilkenny is named.
(from Sanctuary of St Mary's Cathedral, Kilkenny)

ISBN No: 978-0-9928788-4-9
An About Kilkenny Publication
© About Kilkenny
Third edition 2nd printing 2024
Printed by Modern Printers Ltd, Kilkenny

Contents

Kilkenny city seen from the north on a sunny afternoon. St Canice's tower is on the left behind the trees, the Castle is left of centre and St Mary's cathedral is on the right.

Welcome to Kilkenny: Your Invitation

Welcome to Kilkenny, the Medieval heart of Ireland. A city and a county that's a great place to visit and live and also with a great story to tell.

This story has cats, a witch, some knights, Vikings, Cromwell, a Long Man, two parliaments, Santa Claus, saints and scholars, beer, and in more recent times .... hurlers.

It also has big and small castles, round towers, Tudor houses, medieval graveyards, abbeys, churches, a dark cave, a lost town and a pub in a Hole in the Wall.

If that is too grown up for you, you can meet snakes, feed the swans, visit the grave of a long loved doggie, fly on a zip wire, canoe on the river or ride horses.

It has days when you can join the crowd and run in wellies, laugh out loud, feel the rhythm, eat like a king, get artistic or find that long lost book.

For the sporty types, there are fish to catch, horses to back, golf courses to tame, go-karts to race, hills to climb or catch a hurling match, and share in the spirit of Kilkenny.

For a more restful break, there are long walks by the river, drives in the country side, strolls through the woods, gardens to visit, cafes to sit outside, concerts to go to and art to feed the soul.

And if all this is too laid back, there are pubs, restaurants, pubs, shopping, craic, pubs, music, song and dance ...... and pubs.

All this, and more, awaits inside these pages. All that it needs is you and some time to spend in learning or lounging, resting or partying, joining in or crashing out but mostly enjoying your first visit to Ireland's Medieval capital.

James St, leading to St Mary's Cathedral

The stamp above, showing a view of Kilkenny Castle , was issued in 2009 on the 400th anniversary of Kilkenny becoming a city. Reproduced by kind permission of An Post ©

Kilkenny
History

The Irish county of Kilkenny is in the Province of Leinster. At 2,061 sq kms, it is the 16th largest county in Ireland or the 17th smallest, making it the most average sized county on the island.

Its borders are partly formed by the Three Sister river; the Barrow, the Nore and the Suir. The Barrow is on the eastern border, dividing the county from Carlow, and is Ireland's second longest river at 192 km. The third longest, the Suir, is 184 km in length and separates Kilkenny from Waterford on its southern border.

The river most associated with Kilkenny, the Nore, is the country's 5th longest at 140 km. It splits the county down the middle and was important in shaping Kilkenny's place in history.

The county is generally flat. The highest point in the county is Brandon Hill, near Graiguenamanagh. At a modest 515 metres high, it is the 425th highest point in the country.

The county has a population of 99,000 people. Most of these live in the north of the county around the city of Kilkenny but the second largest population in the county is at Ferrybank which forms part of the suburbs to Waterford City in the south and faces the city across the River Suir.

But, other than its physical shape, what is Kilkenny like? One visitor in the 17th century described it as a place of

"Fire without smoke,
Air without fog,
Water without mud,
Land without bog."

This somewhat enigmatic description refers to the smokeless quality of the anthracite coal from Castlecomer, which heated the homes of the natives; the minimal exposure of the county to salt water, as it is inland, so lacking in sea fogs; the limestone paving of Kilkenny city which prevented mud on the streets but allowed access to the river (unusual in Ireland of the time) and the good quality of the land.

Kilkenny can be a cold place, receiving the most number of days with air frost in the country, with an average of 53 days with air frost recorded annually.

The River Nore, with which the county is most associated, starts next door in Co Tipperary, home of the traditional hurling enemy. It travels through part of Co Laois and then through the county to join the River Barrow near New Ross, before entering the sea at Waterford.

Before the Great Famine, the stretch of river between Kilkenny City and Thomastown was home to a variety of water powered industries including saw milling, flax, brewing, woollen mills and marble works. Some of the ruins of the mills are still to be seen at the water's edge.

Since the 18th century, the city has also been home to a brewery, which eventually produced a drink named 'Kilkenny' that has brought the name further around the world. Since the 1960s, there has been a craft and design industry here with an international reputation.

In modern times the city has become a hub for service and tourist industries and the surrounding country side is home to a rural population working some of the country's best farm land.

The city has been the focus for some of the most important changes in Irish history and was important enough be home to two Irish parliaments and to be visited by a number of British kings.

Although Kilkenny City might lack the physical size of many international cities around the world, it beats Kilkenny City, of La Seuer county, Minnesota which, in the last US census had a population of 134. Both cities twinned in 2013.

Even this has more people however than Kilkenny township in New Hampshire, which has a population of 0.

Kilkennys in Australia and Canada have grown up in the cities of Sydney and Alberta.

None has the history of the original.

A Little Bit of History

Kilkenny sits on bedrock primarily composed of limestone, laid down over 400 million years ago. The Ice Age covered this with gravel and shale 18 thousand years ago. Man was a late arriver, probably around 7000 BC. Finds of flints and stone axes show that humans lived here in the Neolithic era. Bronze Age *fulachtai fia* (field kitchens), used for cooking, are to be found around the county.

A bronze age fish trap from 2500 BC was excavated from beneath John's Bridge in the city, giving us one of the first signs of people at this site.

While little remains of pre-Christian Kilkenny, at Kilmogue in the south of the county stands Ireland's tallest dolmen and at Knockroe there is a megalithic passage tomb, still hosting druids in the 21st century at each winter solstice. It is home to the greatest number of carved celtic stones outside of the Boyne valley in Co Meath.

The region was occupied by the Osraighe or 'people of the deer', whose kingdom formed the easternmost part of the modern province of Munster.

The first King was Aengus Osraigh, who ruled in the 2nd Century and his family, which lost and regained its lands over the centuries, remained as rulers until the arrival of the

Aengus Osraigh, 1st King of Ossory.

Formerly on Ossory Bridge, Kilkenny

7000 BC	4000 BC	3500 BC	2,500 BC	100 AD	402
People roam Kilkenny area	Kilmogue Dolmen built	Dunmore Caves created	Man settling in future City area	The Osraighe occupy Kilkenny	St Kieran founds see of Ossory

B.
C.

A.
D.

Norman invaders almost 1,000 years later. In time the King's clan became known as Mac Gillaphadraig, later Fitzpatrick

From the 1st century BC onwards, ringforts were built around where Kilkenny City is now built, but the earliest permanent settlement can be traced back to the 5th Century, when St Kieran, regarded as the first Irish born saint, was an early visitor and he founded a small church by a ford over the river.

Of these years, little physical evidence remains. Houses and churches were built of wood or sod. However, in the 9th century, stone Celtic crosses began to appear and some of the earliest in Ireland are found in the west of the county and are known as the Ossory High Crosses. (see page 74).

The main story starts with St Canice or Cainneach in the 6th century. Like many of the holy men of his time, he was a priest and missionary and a serial founder of monasteries.

A monastery dedicated to him was founded where St Canice's cathedral now stands in the city and the village that grew up around it became known as Cill Chainnigh or Church of Cainneach (Canice).

This remains the Gaelic name for the city

and county and "Kilkenny" is an anglicisation of the name.

Over time, the church adopted the lands of the Osraighe as the Diocese of Ossory, which is mainly comprised of the modern County of Kilkenny and parts of County Laois to the north.

Religious houses, and the communities which grew up around them, became rich in learning and property. The county has a number of round towers from these years, built to reflect the prestige of a church or monastery and were used as belfries.

In time, the settlement attracted Viking raids from the river. In 928, raiders came and massacred the Irish in Dunmore, to the north of the city, and artefacts from this time are still being found.

Kilkenny's next major time of change came soon after the Norman Invasion in 1169. This was a critical moment in the creation of modern Kilkenny.

Domnall Mac Giolla Phádraig was ruler of Osraighe and, with others, deposed Diarmaid Mac Murrough as king of Gaelic Leinster. Mac Murrough fled to England for help. Henry II of England sent troops to support him in reclaiming his throne.

The invasion launched from what is now Wales and focused on south Wexford and especially Waterford. Once they established a beachhead, the Normans, with the modern methods of making war, began to work northwards, into the rich lands of the Osraighe.

Using the system that had worked so well for them elsewhere, the Normans, once in control, began to take over the 'liberated' kingdom of Leinster.

The successful expedition leader, Richard fitz Gilbert de Clare, the Earl of Pembroke, better known in Irish history as Strongbow,

High Crosses from 9th century Ahenny

516	600	650	c800	846	928
St Canice is born	Death of St Canice	Church of St Mullins built	Ossory High Crosses erected	High King of Ireland buried at Kilree	Viking massacre at Dunmore

was soon made Lord of Leinster.

He had a motte and bailey built at Kilkenny near the river ford which was strategically important as it was on a height above an important crossing. A motte was an earthen mound, usually with a wooden castle on top. The bailey was the space around the castle enclosed by a defensive wall.

The Irish burnt his castle to the ground as soon as he left for Dublin. However, their victory was short lived.

The real growth of the modern town started when his son-in-law, William Marshall, decided to make Kilkenny the base for his permanent occupation of South Leinster in 1207. To do this, he did as all good Normans did, building his castle of stone with a deep moat.

In time a town grew beside it and filled the land between Marshall's castle and the bishop's cathedral and a town wall was built to protect the inhabitants and to help control the collection of taxes.

A separate town already had grown around the cathedral, ruled by the bishop. To differentiate between them the town ruled by the Lord was known as Hightown, which included the houses of the Norman newcomers and the castle.

The bishop's town was called Irishtown and the area remains so named to this day.

Initially, the Normans made Kilkenny the capital of Ireland and the first parliament met here in 1293. There were 12 more held here before it eventually moved to Dublin 70 years later.

The 12th and 13th century saw a flurry of building with many abbeys and monasteries appearing across the county. Many were started by William Marshall and his sons, of which he had five. Each inherited his father's title of Lord of Leinster and each died soon afterwards, childless. On the death of the last,

William Marshall

Formerly on Ossory Bridge, Kilkenny

the lands were divided between their five sisters.

Isabell de Clare, who inherited Kilkenny had no male heirs, so the town passed through her daughter Eleanor, who married Hugh le Despenser. Their heirs eventually sold out to the Butler family in 1391 and Kilkenny and its castle remained with them until the 20th century.

1158	1169	1172	1192	c.1202
Jerpoint Abbey is founded	The Normans invade Ireland	Strongbow builds fortress at Kilkenny	William Marshall becomes Lord of Leinster	Building of Canice's Cathedral starts

In 1316 the army of Edward Bruce ravaged the county in his attempted conquest of Ireland. Brother of Robert the Bruce of Scotland, he attacked Gowran, Kells and Callan but by this time Kilkenny had grown big enough to look after itself and he avoided it.

Kilkenny and its people followed the ways of the lords of the castle. These men and their followers were part of the larger European stage. Knights went on crusades. Trade increased with the sale of wool and raw materials paying for imported wines and silks.

In 1324 Kilkenny became notorious with one of the first trials in Europe for witchcraft, when Alice Kyteler, a four time widow, was accused of using poison and sorcery to kill her husbands. (See page 117)

After much political string pulling, Bishop Richard Ledrede managed to get Dame Alice sentenced to death by burning.

Politically well connected, Alice escaped on the eve of being burned at the stake but her maid Petronella, was flogged and burnt in her place. It was the first witch burning in Europe.

Shortly after, the Butler family, who would become important in all aspects of the growth of Kilkenny, became the Earls of Ormond.

Like most of Europe, Kilkenny suffered under the Black Death. As most of the English and Normans lived in stone buildings, they suffered more than the native Irish whose nomadic lifestyle tending cattle, meant their temporary homes, made of sod and mud, provided less chance for plague carrying rats to move in.

One of the more famous chronicles of the Black Death in Ireland and its effects was written by a monk in Kilkenny, Friar John Clyn. In the end he himself became a victim and died, but his writings still speak to us of these times.

As the 14th century advanced, the Normans began to intermarry with the Gaelic Irish and to adopt some of their ways and laws.

In 1367 to stop Norman lords 'becoming more Irish than the Irish themselves', laws were passed at a parliament held here, since known as the Statutes of Kilkenny. These were a form of medieval apartheid.

These Statutes outlawed intermarriage with the Irish, adoption or fostering of Irish children, taking an Irish name or dressing like the Irish and the king's subjects had to learn English, if they had forgotten it.

Most ironically, laws were passed in Kilkenny to outlaw the playing of hurling, a sport which now almost defines modern Kilkenny.

Even though the penalties were severe, the laws were hard to enforce. However, it did begin a process of dividing the two communities with centuries of distrust, misery and oppression resulting.

Although it had lost its parliaments, Kilkenny's strategic importance was marked by visits from Richard II in 1375 and 1399 and the town prospered.

Like most of Northern Europe in the 16th century, the Reformation of the Church touched Kilkenny and its people. One of its outcomes was that the rulers and the ruled had a new type of division in their lives. Not everyone embraced the new religion but, for some, it was an opportunity for advancement and enrichment.

Medieval religious communities were split up and dispersed. Important buildings came under the control of new masters and many religious buildings were sold cheaply into secular hands.

At this time, Ireland was a dangerous and violent place and those who had property and power took care to hold on to what they had. Tower houses were build around the country

1193	1204	1204	1225	1232	1275
Kells Priory founded	Stone castle built in Kilkenny	Duiske Abbey being built	Black Abbey founded	St Francis Friary founded	Building of city walls commences

and Kilkenny has more than its share.

These strong stone houses are scattered around the county, standing sentinel like in fields, and remain as a visible sign of the fear and division that existed, even in loyal areas such as Kilkenny.

For nearly its first 400 years, Kilkenny was governed by a Sovereign and a town council. But the citizens had higher ambitions. If they could achieve city status, they could grow their prestige and their wealth. The first step came on the dissolution of the monasteries, which gave the town council the opportunity to buy the lands of the Dominicans around the Black Abbey and the Franciscans within the town walls. With these came the many out farms the monasteries owned around the countryside.

This allowed the town expand by providing new land for building, paid for by rents from the lands. However, expansion was slow.

To speed things up, the town council looked over the wall to Irishtown and saw a quick way of getting to their goal. While Hightown had a royal charter, secured through its lord, Irishtown had been more lax and no Royal Charter existed. Hightown (as Kilkenny) applied to the king to annex Irishtown.

The king, who needed money for his lavish administration, was happy to sell his permission. Two became one when the combination was granted on 16th October 1608.

Before the ink was dry on the last charter, on 11th April 1609, King James I of England, still in need of money, awarded the town of Kilkenny a Royal Charter, conferring it with the status of a city, with its own mayor; a status which is ferociously guarded by Kilkenny people since.

However, it continued to have two corporations, one for Irishtown and one for

The Charter document of James I to Kilkenny on 11th April 1609, showing a portrait of the King. The Original Charter is kept in the Tholsel with other important charters and civic records detailing Kilkenny's history. A copy is on display n the Medieval Mile Museum. Photo courtesy Kilkenny Borough Council Archives

1293	**1316/17**	**1324**	**1328**	**1348**
First Parliament held in Kilkenny	Army of Edward Bruce ravages Co Kilkenny	Witchcraft trial of Alice Kyteler	James Butler made 1st Earl of Ormond	John Clyn records the Black Death

Hightown, until 1840.

Less than 30 years after becoming a city, religious wars began in England between King Charles I and his Parliament. This ended with the English Civil War.

Much of Ireland was staunchly for the King and James Butler, 12th Earl of Ormond, led the Royalist forces in Ireland. A Protestant, he also sought to break the political power of the Irish Catholic gentry.

The Catholics feared that Ireland would be invaded by anti-Catholic forces from England, and also saw an opportunity to drive the English from the island. They raised an army to fight for their cause.

By 1641, James was besieged in Dublin by Irish Catholic rebels. These were ironically led by many of his Butler relatives, who had remained Catholic.

In 1642, the Irish bishops declared this to be a "just and holy war", words which have plagued communities around the world since time began.

To protect themselves, a "Supreme Council of the Confederation of Catholics" was formed in Kilkenny and a new government for Ireland was formed. All Catholics took an oath of allegiance to Charles I, but also to resist an English (Protestant) take over of the country.

This period is known as the Confederation of Kilkenny and the city became the capital of Ireland for the second time.

As royalists, they did not call the Supreme Council a parliament, as only the king could legally call one. However, it acted in every way like one.

The rebels were supported by Popes Urban VIII and Innocent X, who sent Cardinal Rinuccini, the archbishop of Fermo in Italy, as his nuncio (ambassador) to the new parliament, with arms and money.

Concessions were negotiated with King

Leaders of the Confederation of Kilkenny

Formerly on Ossory Bridge, Kilkenny

Charles I, but in time, he lost his head, literally, and Oliver Cromwell the Lord Protector, came to Ireland to settle the Irish question for once and for all.

After massacres in Drogheda and Wexford, Cromwell took the town of Callan and then besieged Kilkenny in 1650. Suffering from an severe outbreak of plague and significantly outnumbered, after five days, the occupants of the city surrendered, ending Kilkenny's second time as capital of Ireland.

As a royalist, the Earl of Ormond lost the

1367	1375 & 1399	1391	1462	1536	1536
Statutes of Kilkenny passed	Richard II visits Kilkenny	Butlers acquire Kilkenny Castle	Callan Friary founded	Last Parliament in Kilkenny	Henry VIII suppresses abbeys & monasteries

castle and his lands but regained them when Charles II ascended to the throne after Cromwell's death, earning a Dukedom into the bargain. Many other prominent families lost their places. Some, such as the Rothes, never regained their position.

The new Duke started to create the Kilkenny Castle that we see today from the ruin and wreckage of that left by the Cromwellians.

Over the following two hundred years, many new laws, collectively called the Penal Laws, were brought into force by the English parliament, which prevented Irish Catholics from advancement and betterment by restricting religious practice, access to education, ownership of property and careers in the public service.

Balcony window on Rothe House

In the later Williamite Wars, the Butlers backed the winning side. However, a slow decline in the fortunes of its first family and of Kilkenny's political prominence began to settle in.

There were high points. In 1710, John Smithwick started to brew beer at St Francis Abbey, starting what would become one of Ireland's most popular drinks, Smithwicks ale. In more recent years, its offshoot, 'Kilkenny Irish Beer', carries the city's name and fame throughout the world.

With the benefit of the power provided by the flowing River Nore, woollen mills flourished, as did breweries. Kilkenny settled down to a long period of relative peace, with prosperous business people building up the city.

As time passed however, the mills became unprofitable and closed, one by one. The county's economy and prosperity gradually declined.

Meanwhile, throughout the county children were being born who would make a mark on the world at large. One would design the White House, while another would have an American university named after him.

Another would form one of the country's most important educational organisations, the Christian brothers, and in the 19th century, one Kilkenny son would form the Irish Republican Brotherhood (IRB) or The Fenians, a formative organisation that laid the foundations of the successful struggle for Irish independence.

In 1904, Kilkenny won its first All Ireland Hurling title. Remember the Statutes of Kilkenny tried to stop hurling? Well the game continued and the people of Kilkenny always fostered a love for the game.

Although at the start of the 20th century, the county had more cricket clubs than hurling

1582	1594	1609	1642	1650	1661
Shee Alms House built	Rothe House built	Kilkenny becomes a city by charter	Confederation of Kilkenny starts	Cromwell besieges & takes Kilkenny	1st Duke of Ormonde returns from exile

clubs, the game came to dominate and Kilkenny has produced some of the best hurlers in the country in the last 100 years.

Also in 1904, Edward VII made a successful visit to the city, staying in Kilkenny Castle. But the winds of change were starting to blow in Ireland.

Less than 20 years later, the English had left Ireland and civil war troubled the country. Kilkenny suffered less than other parts of the country at this time. However, it lost one of its grandest homes with the burning of Woodstock House at Inistioge in 1922.

During the War of Independence it had housed the infamous Auxiliaries, whose cruel methods made them a hated name in modern Irish history, but it was during the Civil War that followed that the house was destroyed, the day after the Free State troops left it.

Sadly, two Kilkenny men were executed by a Kilkenny firing squad in the city during this time, an inevitable outcome of conflicts that pits neighbours against each other.

In 1935, the Butler family who had lived there for centuries, closed the Castle and left Ireland.

In 1967, the then Marquess of Ormonde sold the Castle to the people of Kilkenny and it has been restored and opened to the public since.

In the 1960s, Kilkenny became the centre for the development of the Irish craft industry. Potters, jewellers, glass makers and other artisans came to the city to open their own workshops and rekindle an interest in their crafts.

As a result, the county is scattered with many successful craft businesses with a world reputation.

In more recent times, the city and county has begun to reconnect with its medieval past. Years of economic poverty meant that the city had not lost all of its historic fabric to developers. Its unique look and charm has made it a destination for visitors.

At the same time, modern businesses such as food and nutrition group Glanbia, which has grown from the co-operative efforts of the local farming community, have seen local employment supported.

Creatively, Kilkenny is home to one of the most successful animation companies outside of Disney. Each of its first four feature length animated films secured an Oscar nomination for best animated film.

Diageo, the owners of Smithwicks Brewery, decided to close it down in 2013 after 300 years and the city has acquired the site on which it was located. The redevelopment of this significant area in the heart of the city holds the prospect of a 21st century Kilkenny beginning to reap the reward of preserving much of its own and Ireland's culture and history.

1710	1761	1843	1845/49	1904	1967
John Smithwick starts to brew beer.	The Tholsel is built.	Building of St Mary's Cathedral starts.	The Great Famine.	Kilkenny wins first All Ireland Hurling trophy.	Castle gifted to Kilkenny.

The Medieval Church building

The Church was all important in Medieval society. Not only was it the direct link to God and the life hereafter, but the bishops, abbots and clergy held temporal power over the people also. Much of the lands were owned either by the Lord and his men or by the Church.

They also controlled rivers, woods and mills, which provided for life, and ran courts which protected its flock or punished transgressors in this life.

There are medieval churches throughout the city and county. While there are many shapes and designs, some parts are common to nearly all.

Churches tended to be built so that the priest and the people would worship in the direction of the Holy Land, the East. The eastern end was called the chancel and contained the altar.

It usually had a large window behind it to let in the morning light. If a community had money, then these windows in time would have been filled with stained glass showing scenes of the bible.

In a monastery monks sat along either side of the altar during mass in an area called the choir.

The nave was the largest part of a church going towards the west, where often the main doorway was located. The people sat or stood in the nave to hear mass.

In some churches, tombs of important people were built along the side of the nave, so that those within were always in the church.

Larger churches had two transepts or arms and the part of the church where the nave, chancel and transepts met was called the crossing. The transepts would usually have side altars and in the really large churches, more altars could be built along the side of the Nave.

Very often a large church had a tower built over the crossing, in which the bells were housed.

Larger churches may have had a Lady Chapel. In a monastery, this was a separate chapel dedicated to the Blessed Virgin.

In a monastery there could have been a number of small chapels where mass could be said by the many priests for the souls of benefactors.

Many churches were built on the foundations of earlier churches and incorporated parts of the old buildings. This led to a mix of architectural styles.

The most high profile remnant of the earlier Irish churches were the round towers, the remains of five of which are scattered around the county of Kilkenny.

East

Chancel

North Transept

Crossing

South Transept

Nave

West

St Canice's Cathedral showing the long nave with the North Transept to the left.

'Void Anchored' by Michael Warren.
This large sculpture found its home in Kilkenny Castle's park in 1985.

Kilkenny City

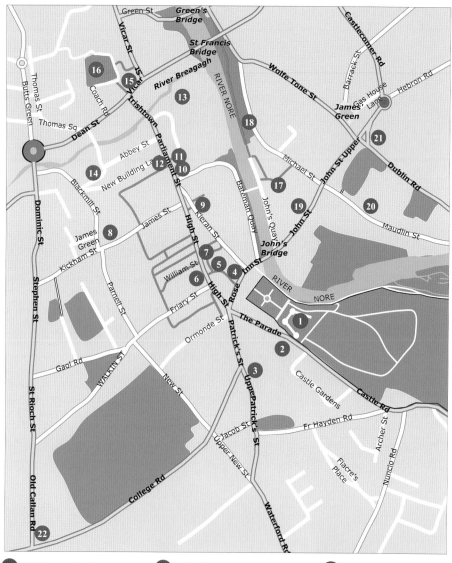

1 Kilkenny Castle	**9** Kyteler's Inn	**17** Butler Gallery
2 Stables & Workshops	**10** Grace's Castle	**18** War Memorial
3 Butler House	**11** Brewery Experience	**19** St. John's Church
4 Shee Alms House	**12** Rothe House	**20** Maudlin St. Tower
5 St. Mary's Church	**13** St. Francis Abbey	**21** Famine Memorial
6 The Hole in the Wall	**14** Black Abbey	**22** Talbot's Tower
7 The Tholsel	**15** St. Canice	
8 St. Mary's Cathedral	**16** St. Canice's Cathedral	

Kilkenny *(Cill Channaigh)*

The heart of the medieval city of Kilkenny is 800m from one end to the other, that is the distance from Kilkenny Castle at the south end of the city to St. Canice's Cathedral at the north.

Along this spine you will experience Ireland's Medieval Mile, a collection of medieval buildings, which taken together paint a picture of the changing political and social fortunes of the city.

Pre-Norman Ireland can be seen in the Ossory High Cross exhibition in the Medieval Mile museum and the tower at St. Canice's Cathedral.

Norman Ireland can be seen with the Castle, the Black Abbey, St. Francis Abbey and St. Canice's Cathedral once more.

Late Medieval Ireland is represented by Rothe House, a merchant's house from the late 16th century.

Georgian Ireland is on display in the streetscape through the town with some fine examples on Parliament St. and the Parade.

Taken together, over 1000 years of the city's history is around you as you wander the streets.

Thus almost all you wish to see is a short stroll from the last place you visited. Strolling the streets is a reward in itself. There you will see a variety of photogenic shop fronts. If this gets tiring, then you will just have to stop and you will find a pub within steps of where you are, where you can meet living Kilkenny, in its people.

The city is well supplied with a wide range of places to eat and attracts foodies to the Savour Kilkenny festival held here each October.

The city boasts one Michelin starred restaurant, *Campagne*, Tel: 056-7772858. Not to be outdone, the county has a second, the *Lady Helen Restaurant* on the Mount Juliet estate near Thomastown. Tel: 056-777 3000.

Many of the businesses are in the hands of local families for generations. As a result, there are still few multi national shops intruding on the Kilkenny character, which shows in the care which the shop owners give to their buildings and windows.

Using this guide will allow you move at your own pace and to follow your own interests. You can wander off course and still be within a short walk of the next place to see.

If you want to get a good overview and be guided through the sights, there are a number of options open to you. See page 141 for a choice of tour options.

In addition to the book telling you about the individual sights in the city, there is a section at the end of this chapter which tells you the story of the town walls, should you want to know more about this part of the city's heritage.

As with all guides, the real world changes daily, leaving the printed word sometimes out of step. The information on opening times included here can change, so please check ahead if there is something you specially want to see.

Kilkenny Tourist Office in High St. is a good place to get a free map, up to date information on the sights, the events and accommodation.

Also useful is the website www.Kilkenny.ie which keeps up to date with everything happening in the city and county.

Overleaf: Aerial photo of Kilkenny Castle, Park, stables and Butler House and gardens.
Courtesy. John Ryan, Pembroke Hotel

① Kilkenny Castle

Kilkenny Castle and Rose Garden

Kilkenny Castle came to be because of one Norman knight - Richard fitz Gilbert de Clare, known in history as Strongbow. He was a leading knight who helped King Henry II of England take control of some parts of Ireland, from 1169 onwards.

Strongbow founded the first wooden motte and bailey buildings of the castle in 1172, overlooking the strategic river crossing below. The site had previously been where the Kings of Osraighe had their residence. The Gaelic Irish burnt down the Normans' replacement the following year.

Strongbow died four years later, and his lands eventually passed to his son-in-law, William Marshall, the true architect of Kilkenny.

Marshall was one of the most successful and fearless of all Norman knights at that time. As a result, he was granted vast portions of captured land. He chose to settle in Ireland, and, in 1207, he established the Medieval town of Kilkenny.

In about 1209, he started to rebuild Kilkenny Castle where the wooden castle had once stood. The stone curtain walls and the round towers were all his work.

Through political manoeuvring, Marshall heirs lost their land and castle and by 1381 it had been seized by King Richard II and was sold to James Butler, 3rd Earl of Ormond, beginning a connection between the Butlers and Kilkenny that lasted for almost 6 centuries.

Marshall's castle had four towers originally. The Eastern wall and the North-Eastern tower were smashed during the siege of the Castle by Oliver Cromwell's troops in 1650. The Castle had major political significance as it was home to the parliament of the Irish Confederacy.

Bombarding it marked Cromwell's dominance over the Confederacy, and hence ultimately of Ireland. In ruins, the wall and tower were later taken away entirely.

A Royalist, James Butler, the 12th Earl, had lost his lands as part of Cromwell's subjugation of Ireland and fled to live in France with Charles II.

On the Restoration of the monarchy, he regained his estates, and the Castle and was made the 1st Duke of Ormonde. He had previously added an 'e' to the end of the family name, now Ormonde, to celebrate being made a Marquess. Inspired by the grand chateaux and palaces he had seen in France, he began to remodel the Castle in their style.

Later generations added to his vision and, as the family became wealthier and styles changed, some of the 1st Duke's chateaux ideas were demolished and an idealised romantic medieval style was brought in.

Building the gate in the 13th century wall facing out towards the city street was from this time.

As a result, the castle has become a muddle of architectural styles. Long windows at ground level facing on to formal gardens were never in the original Norman plans.

Cromwell wasn't the only one to besiege Kilkenny Castle. In 1922, Ireland was heading towards Civil War. Lord and Lady Ossory (Butlers) were living in the Castle.

One May morning at 5:30 am, His Lordship's butler woke him to say that anti-Treaty Republican forces had seized his castle. With a stiff upper lip, both the Lord and his Lady stayed put, despite the arrival an armed body of men.

Shortly after, troops from the Irish Free State army laid siege to the occupied castle, containing his Lordship and his Lady, their servants and Pekinese dogs and 22 rebels.

The Butlers barricaded themselves in their bedroom while a two day siege took place outside the door. In the end the Free State forces crashed a car into the castle adding to the damage of the previous two days. They claimed credit for releasing Lord and Lady Ossory. Some time later, the anti-Treaty forces claimed to have been their protectors in the siege.

The depressed economy of the new Ireland was not kind to the Butler family. By 1935, they decided that the time had come to leave the Castle, as they could no longer afford to keep it.

They sold the contents in an auction which took 10 days and moved to London. The castle lay unoccupied and fell into disrepair. For the next 30 years, it decayed rapidly - a sad, abandoned and uninhabited ruin.

In the 1960s, the Butlers finally got round to selling the place to the people of Kilkenny for a nominal sum of £50, in recognition of the building's historical importance to the country.

Since then efforts are made to buy back any of the original furnishing and contents when they turn up at auctions in Ireland or abroad.

The building is now held and managed by the Office of Public Works on behalf of the people of Ireland.

THE GATEWAY

The facade is flanked by the West Tower to he left and the Parade Tower to the right. They remain as dominant and striking as they must have been when originally built, but the later addition of windows shows how the function of the

building changed over the centuries from defence to luxurious living.

The gateway from the main street is flanked outside by the remains of a moat or dry ditch which had been filled in the 17th century but has recently been excavated.

The right hand ditch has a small postern gate that allowed entrance to the castle through the thick and heavily sloped wall.

The gateway is a late addition, being finished in 1710 with later decorations added in the passing years. The walls in which the gateway stands once contained a residence for the gatekeeper but now contain offices.

THE COURTYARD

Entering by the main gate you come to what could have been an enclosed area in the original castle and is now a manicured lawn open at one side to a sweeping view of the Castle park.

Three wings of the building enclose the courtyard. The wing facing the gate as you enter is a replacement for the original. When rebuilding, the upper floor was designed to hold a long and imposing picture gallery. The lower windows gave light to what were the servant quarters but which now houses the Butler Gallery, one of Ireland's leading public art galleries.

The wing facing the parkland has three tiers of windows giving light to most of the formal rooms of the residence. These are topped by an array of upright chimneys, never part of the original vision of the first medieval designer. The entrance to the castle is on the ground floor.

The Gateway wing is bracketed by the West Tower and the Parade Tower. Flanking the doors to this part of the building and over the gateway are stone heads, which were late additions to the original building. Some of the drainpipes have decorative lead rainwater heads with the date 1682 inscribed. However, most are later replicas.

The Parade Tower is used as a conference centre and for lectures, concerts and other public functions. There is a free audio visual display on the castle in the ground floor of the tower which gives a good overview of the history, the people and the building.

Just beyond the Parade Tower are some steps leading underground. These were used by the servants to enter and leave the building, so that they would not upset the lives of their employers upstairs by being seen.

INSIDE THE CASTLE

A 12th century castle redesigned in the 19th century and set in large parklands, the castle has served as the principal seat of the Butler family, Earls, Dukes and Marquesses of Ormonde for over six centuries.

It now includes a library, drawing room, and bedrooms decorated in 1830s ornate style, plus the fine Long Gallery.

Inside the building, the entrance corridor runs the length of one side of the courtyard. Turning right brings you, at the end of the corridor, to steps down to visit the Butler Gallery and the kitchens where a bustling cafe is now located.

There are tours of the Castle which are well worth taking as knowledgeable guides seem to know everything about the castle and its inhabitants.

Passing the ticket office, and going down under the Rose Garden Terrace is a flight of steps which leads you under the West Tower. Here you can see part of the base of the tower and foundations which gives one a feeling of the size of the undertaking in building the original castle.

The Tower room itself has a wattle and daub ceiling from the late medieval period with the imprint of the willow branches which helped form it very visible. The thickness of the massive walls show the seriousness with which the designer took the danger of attack.

The main floors above come from a different time. This is a castle of a rich family of the 19th century. The main work started in 1830 and the style and decoration of the time is evident everywhere.

The purpose and names of rooms changed over time. The ground floor contains the Chinese withdrawing room, where ladies went after dinner so that men could enjoy their own company, the State Dining Room and the main entrance hall.

The State Dining Room has a formal dinner table laid out, with a portrait of James the 1st Duke, painted by Sir Peter Lely, overseeing the empty chairs.

The floor of the entrance hall has a chess board appearance and highlights Kilkenny Marble in the black squares and local sandstone for the rest. The walls show the portraits of Earls and Dukes from the family's past.

The stairs to the upper floors leads to a keyhole shaped room which once had walls hung with tapestries. These are under restoration. There are some bullet holes beneath one window which were made when the castle was under attack in 1922.

The upper floor contains the family rooms which are no less grand. Outside the Library at the top of the stairs are displayed two parchments, which trace the family tree back to 1066. A very important item for a noble family to have.

Much work went into furnishing the rooms on this floor in as close a way possible to how they looked at their prime, with wallpapers and carpets made to designs found by research and good luck.

The Library and Drawing Room look stuffy to the modern eye but would have been the height of luxury at the time. This would have been needed as the castle was host to visits by Butler relations from across Europe, some of whom would have been from royal families in their own countries.

The third floor in this block has a long corridor painted in blue with bedrooms opening off it. This corridor once housed an impressive art collection, now sadly scattered around the globe.

The third tower looks over the River Nore. At the top of the tower is the bedroom with the best view and this was where King Edward VII stayed when he visited in 1904. Outside the door is the first flush toilet, installed specially for the Kings visit.

Close by is the Moorish staircase. The design is very different to the rest of the building but it served a useful purpose in providing access in an awkward part of the building as well as letting in much needed light.

Down these stairs you are brought to the door of the Long Gallery.

THE LONG GALLERY

The Picture Gallery Wing was built during the early 19th-century by William Robertson, and was built on earlier foundations. He built in the same castellated baronial style as the rest of the castle. Initially the gallery had a flat roof, but this began to cause problems shortly after its completion.

In the 1860s, two other architects, Sir Thomas Newenham Deane and Benjamin Woodward, made changes to the overall design of the Gallery. These included inserting four oriel windows in the west wall, while blocking up eight existing windows and adding another oriel in the east wall. A pitched roof was put in place, with central glazing.

The hammer-beam roof is worth as much attention as many of the paintings hanging in the gallery. This roof is supported on carved stone corbels and the ceiling was decorated by John Hungerford Pollen, then Professor of Fine Arts at Newman College, Dublin. He used a mix of quasi-mediaeval and pre-Raphaelite styles, with interlace, gilded animal and birds' heads on the cross beams.

This room itself is 36m (120 ft) long and was once filled with paintings and sculptures. It gives you an idea of the wealth of the family and its ambitions at the time it was built in the early nineteenth century.

The centre of the left hand wall is dominated by a large Carrara marble fireplace decorated with beautiful carvings. Among these are scenes showing the purchase of the castle in 1391 by the then Earl, Richard II being offered wine by the Chief Butler and, as good public relations spin, a lady of the family giving food to the poor, of whom there would have been plenty.

The Gallery now contains a number of paintings, well short of the number held when the family was at its most prominent. There are some portraits of former Earls and family members. The original collection can never be put together again.

Photo: © National Monuments Service. Dept of Arts, Heritage and the Gaeltacht.

Castle Park & Gardens

Kilkenny Castle is located in parklands which span almost 20 ha (50 a). The formal ornamental rose garden is on the city side of the castle and its formality mirrors the stern tight facade of the castle looking down on it. The garden is laid out in the shape of a Celtic cross with the castle at its base.

Looking down on the gardens are two statues; one of Hermes, after an original in the Vatican Collection and the other is of Diana the Huntress.

A good view of the river and the east of the city can be had from the viewing point at the end of the path crossing before the castle.

The wings of the castle open out on its other side onto a large expanse of parkland which is a playground for the city. Many weekends throughout the year there are events held here for national and local bodies.

The cast iron gates at the entrance beside the Parade Tower originally came from St. Stephens Green in Dublin. The outer perimeter walk is 1.2 km long and gives walkers sights of wildlife, with wild squirrels aplenty.

At the farthest point of the park is the ornamental lake, with ducks and swans swimming calmly. Nearby is the massive sculpture '*Void Anchored*' (see page 12).

The park also has a playground for children, suitable for 2 to 10 year olds. Older children play ball on the open parkland and throughout the summer local children can be seen playing with their hurleys,

The park is a regular haunt for walkers and runners and has a number of picnic tables for families who enjoy their food *al fresco.*

There is a shorter paved walk which takes in half of the park and walking this you pass a small graveyard containing the graves of some Marquesses and Marchionesses of the Butler family. At the rear of the small cemetery and outside the railings is the grave of Sandy, a much loved pet.

Beside the cemetery is a modern sculpture to commemorate those who have disappeared in Ireland and shows the loss through the symbol of the searching hands of the relatives they have left behind.

Opening times: the park is open daily year round, Open from 8:30am to 8.30pm in summer, 9am to 4.30pm in winter.

> The highest temperature ever recorded in Ireland was 33.3°C (91.9 °F) at Kilkenny Castle on 26 June 1887.

www.kilkennycastle.ie
Opening hours
Oct - Mat.   09.30 - 17.00
April - Sept   09.30 - 17.30

Admission charges apply. The tour of the castle can be self guided. Guided tours are available and can be booked in advance.

There is a coffee shop on the grounds.

The Stables & The Workshops

Facing the main gates of Kilkenny Castle are the lordly stable yards, built by the 17th Earl in 1790. With its crescent-shaped building, circular windows and copper-domed tower, it was very impressive and housed the Duke's horses better than many of the people in the district. As the Castle fell into disuse, so also did the stables.

In 1965 these buildings were converted to house Kilkenny Design Workshops (KDW), a state-sponsored project aimed at improving the design of Irish products and increasing exports.

Designers from across Europe were employed as lead designers and five workshops opened - silver and metalwork, textile weaving, textile printing, ceramics and woodworking.

KDW closed in 1983, however many of the original designers stayed and established studios in the area. Today the Castle Yard is owned by Kilkenny Civic Trust and is home to a number of thriving craft and design businesses where it is possible to watch skilled craftspeople at work.

It was here in the workshop of James Kelly that the current Liam McCarthy cup was made in 1992. Awarded to the winners of the senior All Ireland Hurling Championship, the Kilkenny team has been the most frequent winner of the new trophy since.

The Yard is also home to the National Craft Gallery in whose showrooms important craft exhibitions are held.

You enter the Yard through an arched gateway spanned by the Kilkenny Design Centre, whose timber-beamed ceilings and stone walls contain a busy restaurant serving delicious freshly cooked and baked Irish food and an extensive craft shop featuring Irish-made products.

Inside the Castle Workshop Yard

③ Butler House

The Castle Yard links from Kilkenny Castle itself, to the beautifully-restored walled garden of Butler House, the Georgian Dower House of the Castle, accessed from the rear of the Yard, opposite the main entrance.

When the Lord of the Castle died, his widow left to make way for the heir and his wife. She retired to live in the Dower house. Butler house was built for this purpose.

It has not always been a place for the nobility and functioned as a soup kitchen in 1832, during a cholera outbreak in the city.

The house is now a guest house and is also used for conferences and weddings. The gardens are open to the public from 9am to 5pm daily.

On March 8th 1966, a large bomb blew up Nelson's Pillar in the centre of Dublin. This 37m high column was surmounted by a statue of Horatio Nelson and was a symbol to many of historic English rule. It was erected in 1809, 30 years before the one in Trafalgar Square in London.

The stones around the pond in the gardens are some of the last remaining fragments of this iconic structure. These formed the plinth on top on which Nelson's statue stood. Names of some of his victories were carved around this and you can still form the names of St. Vincent and Copenhagen from the pieces.

One of the fragments from Nelson's Pillar now decorating the gardens of Butler House

25

The Parade

The large open plaza between the Castle and the city is the known as the Parade. On the castle side is a graveled walkway and taking this side gives you the opportunity to admire the Georgian buildings on the other side of the space. Sadly, there is a modern intrusion which spoils the streetscape, but is does give an idea of the wealth and position which the town had gained for itself in the early 18th century.

On Thursday mornings each week a small but busy farmer's market is held here, adjacent to the castle.

From the Parade you will also see the spire of St. Mary's Cathedral. At the end of the Parade, the street to the right, called Rose Inn St. after a long gone Inn of that name, leads down to Shee Alms house.

4 Shee Alms House

This Tudor building was built in 1582 by Sir Richard Shee, a rich lawyer. One of the panels over the front door shows his coat of arms and the date the place was built.

He acquired a great deal of church property at the time of the Reformation, probably to prevent it from falling into the hands of reformers and he was known to be a very religious man.

With the dissolution of the existing church, no provision was made for continuing the charitable work it did.

Shee's plan was to house a hospital in the building. Called the Hospital of Jesus of Kilkenny, it was to house six male and six female paupers. Sir Richard gave them money each week for food, clothing and fuel. He paid

for medical help and for their burial. He died in 1608.

In his will, he said that if the house was passed away from the family the relatives would be cursed. This curse may explain why the family made great efforts to keep the house in the family down through the years.

After the arrival of Cromwell and the Penal Laws, the Shees, as Catholics themselves, became poor when they were dispossessed of their property.

Many generations later in 1756, the family recovered the house through a descendant living in France and he re-endowed it, but bad luck hit again as he fell foul of the French revolution and payments to keep it open stopped.

A further descendant took it up once more some years later and it continued to look after the poor until 1895 when it eventually closed.

In 1928, reconstruction work started and continued fitfully until the local authority took it over in 1978 and restored it to its original condition.

Little of the internal fittings remain but it is one of the few remaining Tudor alms houses in Ireland and a monument to the Shee family whose charitable gift still stands over 400 years later.

The room upstairs opens on to St. Mary's Lane at the rear, which leads you to St. Mary's churchyard.

Until 2019, it was Kilkenny's tourist office but since this moved, the premises remains closed to the public.

High St.

High St. is a short 350m long road joining the Parade to the junction of Parliament St. and Kieran St. In Medieval times, this was the centre of the town, which in time extended further towards the Cathedral to the north.

Off the street to the right at 100m is a side lane which leads to St. Mary's Church and graveyard. Opposite this junction is the entrance to the Hole in the Wall. *(page 30)* The main building you see is the Tholsel *(page 31)* which juts out into the street.

Beyond the Tholsel is the Butter Slip, a short lane joining High St. with Kieran St. Another shorter slip is further up the street.

To the left of the street is the first of the many narrow lanes which ran beside the properties to the old city walls. Some now provide access to delivery entrances to shops. One, Chapel Lane, leads up to Wellington Square, a small enclave of Georgian houses.

St. Mary's & the Medieval Mile Museum

This small church sits at the junction of some of the medieval lanes of Kilkenny. It is reached by the narrow lane a few doors up the street from the tourist office or from High St. by the lane next to Goods department store.

St. Mary's church viewed from Rose Inn St.

St. Mary's was the church for the burgesses and merchants of Kilkenny. St. Canice's to the north was the church for the lords and the gentry.

Although no longer a place of worship, it was one of the most in demand churches in Kilkenny during its long life. In the beginning, the wealthiest of burgesses were allowed to be buried within the church while everyone else had to make do with the churchyard.

Outside was not desirable. In 1337, an ordinance was passed which rewarded anyone who killed pigs found within the churchyard.

Throughout the middle ages the town council maintained the church and graveyard and an annual four pence was collected from each hall and a 1s 2d from each stall or shop to fund its upkeep.

Originally built in 1202, with a tower added in 1343, it served the Catholic community until the Reformation, when it became a Protestant house of worship.

In 1603, after the death of Elizabeth I, the Catholics took it back and re-dedicated it. This did not last for long as the Protestants took it back before James I re-established the Protestant church more firmly in Ireland.

Then the Catholics took it back once more, when Kilkenny became the seat of the parliament of the Catholic Confederates against the English Parliament, with no less than Cardinal Rinuccini, the Papal Nuncio (ambassador) doing the re-dedication. However, the confederation lasted only a short

27

few years and finally, the Protestants got the church back for good.

The church building underwent modification throughout the medieval period. Renovations in 1739 incorporated much of the medieval fabric. The chancel was demolished in 1748 and the bell tower was repaired in 1774. This tower was later replaced in 1819-20 by a tower at the west end.

The church closed in the late 1950s as a place of worship and was recently taken over by the Local Authority for the people of Kilkenny. The church is now a public museum, to display the city's treasures.

The adjacent graveyard contains the largest collection and some of the finest Renaissance-style and later tombs in the country.

To be buried here was a privilege. Centuries of bones lie beneath the surface, many from the merchant and ruling families. Their ornate tombs are all that is now left of many of them.

After years of neglect, these tombs are now receiving the care and restoration needed to bring them back to their former glory.

> In the 17th Century, the Corporation laid down some rules for important funerals here:
> "Orders for burials—That the sword and four maces shall be carried before the Mayor at the burial of Aldermen and their wives; and that those that are to be buried at St. Mary's church shall be carried in at the west gate; and if any howling or crying be at any such burial, the Mayor and company to withdraw till they leave off howling."

Tomb Weepers on the Shee Family tomb. From the left: James the Great, Thomas, James the Just, Philip, Bartholomew, Jude, Matthias. Photo: Cóilín Ó Drisceoil / Kilkenny Archaeology ©

Interior of the Medieval Mile Museum. Showing the Kilkenny Room through the large arched windows in the far wall and the open roof trusses above.

Opening Hours: Tuesday to Sunday 9:30am to 4:30pm.   Closed Mondays.
Entrance fee applies. www.medievalmilemuseum.ie Tel: 056-7817022

6 The Hole in the Wall

Kilkenny has had two buildings called 'The Hole in the Wall", the more famous being a tavern which existed off High St.

The building was built in Tudor times by the Archer family. In those times, burgesses tended to build second inner houses for an older child on the land at the rear of the existing home and that is what happened here.

A plaque on the wall above O'Connors Jewellers at No 18, shows it is the site of Archers house. The house was much wider than the current shop fronts and spanned No 18 and No 19. The family crest can still be seen in the wall over the Georgian doorway in the centre of the three shops.

A barred gateway to the left of No 17 leads to the second home at the rear. Hemmed in now by more recent buildings, it still retains an air of Elizabethan merchant wealth.

The building is typically Tudor in style, with a tall pitched roof, cut-stone hooded Elizabethan mullioned windows, original flagstones, hexagonal chimney and oak doors.

The ground floor is divided into a rustic tavern made from 1582 oak beams, floor boards and other original oaks. Outside, there is a moderate sized enclosed courtyard.

An upper floor with a small gallery gives a flavour of how it would have been when the Archers lived there.

Like many wealthy Catholics in Kilkenny, the arrival of Cromwell saw the Archers lose what they owned in 1654 and their houses passed to the Duke of Ormonde who rented them out. In time, the house at the rear housed a famous tavern.

To enter it separately from the house at the front, a hole was punched in an adjacent wall and the legend of the "Hole in the Wall" was born.

'If you ever go to Kilkenny,
look out for the Hole in the Wall,
where you'll get blind drunk for a penny
and tipsy for nothing at all'.

It has hosted many of the city's famous visitors from Henry Grattan, Thomas Moore and the young Duke of Wellington.

Hidden from view, in time the building fell into disuse and was rescued by a local enthusiast in 1999 when he started to renovate and restore the building. It opens to the public, during the summer and for music and artistic events.

With a modern liquor licence, the building is once more fulfilling its purpose, serving the city as it has for many centuries.

Hidden behind the buildings off High St. and buried among later buildings, 'The Hole in the Wall' has survived for over 400 years.

7 The Tholsel

The fine stone building which dominates High Street, not only by its height, but by prominently butting out into the street, is the Tholsel. It presents a strong image with the thick stone columns around an open arcade.

The exact meaning of the word is uncertain but may be from the old English words for tax hall.

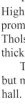

Tholsels have been used as town halls, jails, council houses, custom halls and guild halls, and Kilkenny's example was no different. The present building is the third in the city and is built on the site of the second which was built around 1582.

Before the current building was erected, the Market Cross was here. This is where market stalls would have been put up on market and fair days.

It was here on November 3rd 1324, that one of the first witch burnings in Europe took place.

In later years, mystery plays were performed here and later an open air theatre existed.

Even today, singers and buskers often occupy the open arcade area for shelter and the echoing sound from the stone surroundings.

The current building was erected in 1761 using local unpolished marble and limestone at a cost of £1,315. Today it is home to the offices of the Mayor of the city.

Some of the city's most important

documents are kept here, including the all important Charter granted by King James 1st in 1609, as well as the Corporation Sword and Mace (left).

Over the arch leading down High St. is a carved coat of arms of the City Corporation. (see page 13).

The three tier octagonal clock tower, which caps the roof, suffered in a severe fire in 1985 but has been completely restored, preserving one of the city's iconic buildings for posterity.

> The deed for the purchase of the Thosel site dated 20th August 1582 is held in the building.
> The site is owned by the town subject to an annual rent of £1 13s 4d to the heirs of Thomas and William Marshall.

8 St. Mary's Cathedral

From almost every point of the compass, the roads leading into the city show a skyline dominated by the tower of St. Mary's Cathedral.

Built on the city's highest point, the 57 meter (186ft) tower, with its pointed spires reaching skywards, is one of the iconic images of Kilkenny. The tall tower was originally intended to be built for the seminary of St. Kieran's College nearby.

St. Mary's is the Roman Catholic cathedral for the city and St. Canice's is that of the Church of Ireland. It is also called the church of St. Kieran as well as the Cathedral of the Assumption.

On James St, St. Mary's was built by Bishop William Kinsella starting in 1842. The bishop oversaw a boom in church building during his tenure, building 19 churches in the diocese during his time.

St. Mary's Cathedral, viewed from the south.

The Cathedral was designed by William Deane Butler. Work began in February 1842 and continued until 1857.

It cost £25,000, which was paid for by the local population. When one considers that this covered the period of the Great Famine in Ireland, years of immigration, coffin ships, starvation and despair, the people must have felt in need of more than physical nourishment at the time.

Kilkenny was not immune to this tragedy, but people still saw an investment in the cathedral as important to them and their community.

The building is made from cut-limestone which was sourced locally. The cathedral has a cruciform plan and its style is described as Early English Gothic. The design is inspired by the 11th century cathedral in Gloucester, England.

Apart from the massive Gothic facade, it has an Italian marble high altar with relics of St. Cosmos and St. Damian beneath it. It also has a sculpture of the Madonna by Italian artist Giovanni Maria Benzoni.

In the south (left) transept there is a small altar, underneath which is displayed a wax model of St. Victoria, a third century Martyr, containing her bones.

Facing St. Victoria's altar, the Sacred Heart altar, statue and altar rails are credited to the marble works of James Pearse, father of Padraig Pearse, one of the leaders of the 1916 Rebellion.

The Main Altar and Sanctuary of St. Mary's Cathedral

On the end wall of the north (right) transept are two panels listing the names of the bishops of Ossory from St. Kieran's time. The changing names, from Gaelic to Norman to more modern times, chart the changes in the background of the people of Kilkenny.

The Cathedral is due for extensive renovation and the first step was the refurbishment of the adjacent Chapter House which contains a small shop for religious goods and a tea rooms.

The upper floor, which is free to visit, was the meeting place for the bishop and his priests. Restored to its original condition, it contains a dais at one end where the senior members of the Chapter would have sat. The walls are decorated in reproductions of the original design recovered from photos.

The diocesan chapter no longer needs the grandeur of these surroundings for its regular meetings.

The wax figure containing the entire relics of St. Victoria

St. Victoria was promised in marriage to Eugenius, a rich heathen nobleman but she refused either to marry him or to sacrifice to his idols.

Her lover was so angry at her for refusing him that he gave her up to the authorities as a Christian and a dagger was plunged into her heart at his request.

The legend is that her executioner, Lilicarus, was immediately struck with leprosy, and died six days later, eaten by worms.

A sad and gruesome ends for saint and sinner.

Kieran St. & the Slips

Kieran St. runs roughly parallel to High St. and is linked by the Butter Slip and Market Slip, two of the city's medieval lanes. The Butter Slip (see right), which is adjacent to the Tholsel, was once home to a market for butter sellers.

With its arched entry, narrow, dark walkway and the rough stonework of the walls, it can, at quiet moments, let you travel back in your mind to former times. However, it is unlikely this was ever a quiet passageway and buskers in modern days uphold that tradition.

At the end of the Slip is Kieran St. To the left are a number of cafes with seating on the street to let you see the world pass by and the world to look at you.

⑨ Kyteler's Inn

At the north end of Kieran St. is Kyteler's Inn, site of the home of one of medieval Europe's most infamous women, Dame Alice Kyteler. Dame Alice was subject to one of Europe's first witch trials, which ended in savagery.

Her home is now a pub and restaurant. With the family name long gone from the city, the Inn is all that remains of her name.

Read the thrilling story of Dame Alice and her maid Petronella of Meath on page 117.

At the rear, in the beer garden, is the covered entrance to St. Kieran's Well. It was beside this well that St. Kieran, the city's patron saint, built his first church.

Kyteler's Inn as seen from Kieran St.

Parliament St.

Parliament St. starts at the junction of High St. and Kieran St. and continues to the Watergate bridge before Irishtown.

Formerly known as the Coal Market, it was here that the carts from the coal mines of Castlecomer, 15km to the north, came to sell fuel to the city dwellers.

Its name was later changed to Parliament St. as it was here that the building which housed the Assembly of the Confederation of Kilkenny stood. Effectively, it was the rebel's parliament house. Nothing of it remains.

A plaque on a pillar, by the traffic lights at the entrance to the Market Yard beside the Bank of Ireland, marks where it stood.

The street is home to Grace's Castle, the Brewery museum and Rothe House. Access to the Black Abbey is by Abbey St., on the left opposite the Watergate Theatre.

Just beyond the theatre to the right is the site of the former Smithwicks brewery, where the last remains of St. Francis Abbey still stands. The area is now under redevelopment.

The lower end of the street has a very high number of pubs adjoining each other. Grouped together almost directly opposite the old brewery gates, it would seem that the act of brewing generated a great thirst among the workers such as could not wait to be quenched.

New Building Lane. One of the lanes that joined Parliament St. to the original town wall

10 Grace's Castle - The Court House

Located on Parliament St., this fine building has sat back from the street for 800 years. The original building was erected by William le Gros (modernised as Grace) in 1210 but the only remains, other than the name, are the foundations in the basement.

The family lost the castle in 1566 and the building became a prison. In 1794, it became a courthouse, which it remains today.

It was before this building that many unfortunate rebels from the 1798 rebellion were executed.

The seven bays at street level are suggestive of prison cells, for which they may have been used.

The current building is early 19th century design and a more modern extension extends down to the adjacent Market Yard.

The long balcony facing Parliament St. was used for making speeches at large political gatherings in the 19th century but in the late 20th century it was used to welcome victorious county hurling teams home with the All Ireland Senior and Minor hurling and camogie trophies.

The Court House was the location of the county gaol until the early 19th century when a new purpose built gaol was built on the edge of the city to serve the region.

Its courtyard was the scene of one of the last cases of pressing to death in the British Isles.

In August 1740 Matthew Ryan was brought before the court accused of highway robbery. When he refused to plead he was sentenced to suffer *peine dure et forte*.

This meant he was laid on the ground and his arms and legs were stretched and tied to posts. Then heavy stones and bars of metal were placed on his chest.

This had the effect of slowly crushing his chest until he agreed to plead. He survived two days until he died.

11 Smithwick's Experience

Beside Grace's Castle is a fine Georgian building which today houses the Smithwick's Experience. This tells the story of brewing in Kilkenny and of the Smithwick family whose beer has carried the name of Kilkenny around the world.

Beside the building is an arch leading down to one of the original gates of the brewery, which grew up on the abbey lands behind it, and is the entrance to the Experience today.

Brewing has been carried out on the abbey site for almost 800 years. The monks brewed beer for themselves.

As fasting was part of a monk's life, days without food were

Home of the Smithwick's Experience.

common. However, they found a substitute in beer made from barley, which was liquid bread. With the river beside them and fields to grow the barley and hops, the monks had plenty of practice at getting the brew just right.

Although the monks eventually left, brewing was now established in Kilkenny, with a brewery started on the old abbey lands. In the early 1700's, John Smithwick (the 'w' is silent) joined the business. A catholic, he had to remain a silent partner and from 1710, a silent owner.

The business grew, selling tea as well as beer. John began to buy up adjoining pieces of land he needed to expand the business. Sadly, when John died, the family sold the brewery.

His grandson, Edmund, bought the brewery back in 1827 and took over where his grandfather left off. The business grew and the beer, now with the family name on the label, was exported.

By the mid-19th century a large brewery was in place on the site. It lasted for over a century until, in 1964, a new brew house was built and Arthur Guinness & Son became involved soon after. Further modernisation continued until a twenty-first century, computer-operated brewery came into being.

Smithwick's Brewery has brewed ale for over three centuries. It is a clear beer with a chestnut colour and a creamy head. More recently developed is 'Kilkenny Irish Cream Ale' which is a deeper red in colour.

Sadly, the brewery has closed its operations in the city. The 20a site, which it occupied, contains what is left of the original Franciscan abbey. It is currently being developed by the Local Authority for the benefit of the city.

Original gate to Smithwick's Brewery

Opening Hours: Every day all year round. Hours vary by season. Entry fee applies. Pre-book tickets on www.smithwicksexperience.com. Tel: 056-778 6377

12 Rothe House

Past Grace's Castle on the opposite side of Parliament St. is Rothe House, a unique Irish early 17th century merchant's townhouse complex built by John Rothe Fitz-Piers between 1594 and 1610. Already a wealthy man from trading in fine cloths, the new house was a visible mark of prestige and position for him.

The Rothes were great merchants and were one of the 10 great families who controlled Kilkenny throughout the 15th and 16th centuries, and into 17th century.

John's wife Rose was a member of the Archers, another prominent family, whose home you may have visited at the 'Hole in the Wall'.

The first house and its courtyard were built in 1594. The building style is English Renaissance.

A shield bearing John's coat of arms — an oak tree and a deer, with the arrow points of the Archers — can still be seen over the entrance archway.

The Rothes were involved in politics and were on the Catholic side in the Confederation of Kilkenny. The bishop of Kilkenny at the time was David Rothe and the family house was used as a meeting place by the Assembly of Bishops.

After the fall of Kilkenny to Oliver Cromwell in 1650, the house was confiscated and the family exiled to Connacht.

Medieval towns were made up of burgage plots, long narrow strips of land between the street and the town walls. A family would build an imposing house facing the street.

When other family members married, either the existing house was extended or a new independent house was built behind the first, with access through it to the street.

John Rothe chose the latter solution. The Rothes built three three-storied houses in total, each with its own enclosed courtyards and still had room for a garden with an orchard behind them.

The building had many uses in the intervening years to the late 20th century, housing families and businesses. At one stage in the 1880s, the courtyards were used to keep pigs for a local butcher.

It fell into disrepair over time and by the end of the 19th century, two of the houses had lost their roofs. In 1890, some work to restore what was lost began.

The front house became a school and Thomas MacDonagh, one of the signatories of the Irish Proclamation of Independence in 1916, taught Irish classes there. (see page 63)

The building remained in a sad state until 1962, when Kilkenny Archaeological Society in a visionary move, bought the property and the recovery of a jewel of Kilkenny's and Irish heritage began.

Rothe House is a rare surviving example in Ireland of such a complex of houses, still retaining the burgage plot and the original town wall at the rear. Today Rothe House contains a private museum which highlights the history of Kilkenny. It is also the home of Kilkenny Archaeological Society and a genealogy centre.

The gardens at the rear have been recreated as they would have looked in the 17th century with plants, herbs and vegetables that would have been common at the time and a separate orchard.

Today it is patrolled by five happy ducks, part of whose function is to keep the slugs and snails under control, as well as police the visitors.

Opening Hours: Tuesday to Sunday from 10:30am to 4pm. Closed Mondays.
www.rothehouse.com Tel:: 056 772 2893

The inner garden of Rothe House in spring.   *Photo Courtesy of Rothe House Trust*

13 St. Francis Abbey

Past the Watergate Theatre in Parliament St., just before crossing the River Breagagh into Irishtown, the street veers to the right towards the entrance to the former Smithwick's Brewery, now closed.

Inside the gates stands the forlorn skeleton of the chancel and bell tower of the church of St. Francis Abbey, which was one of the large monasteries which once formed the backbone of Kilkenny society.

The Franciscan friars came to Ireland around 1226 and St. Francis Abbey was founded sometime around 1231. In spite of its name, it was a Friary, being home to an Order of Friars.

It was founded by Richard Marshall, whose brother William the Younger had founded the Black Abbey nearby.

It was located at the north eastern corner of the medieval Hightown of Kilkenny. Deeper inside the brewery grounds are the remains of Evan's Turret, which formed one end of the city walls. Unfortunately, it is not accessible to the public at present.

The abbey started as a small rectangular chapel and grew over the next 300 years, reaching out from the city walls. This expansion was rapidly halted with the dissolution of the monasteries in the sixteenth century.

In 1543, three years after its dissolution, the abbey was given by royal grant to Walter Archer, sovereign of the city, and in 1550 the friars were expelled.

They came back to the city during the reign of Queen Mary but were again expelled when Elizabeth I took the throne.

Over time, the friars managed to get back to Kilkenny and by the time of the Confederation in 1640, were firmly back in residence. They remained part of the community of Kilkenny until 1829 but never recovered the monastery lands nor the abbey church.

The abbey site housed a military barracks by 1698 and the buildings fell into ruins. In 1849, one visitor noted that the remains of the church were being used as a tennis court. By 1889, the property was taken into public hands.

In 1710, a brewery started on the site but, after 300 years it has now closed. The 20a site which it occupies has been bought by the city. It contains what is left of the original Franciscan abbey.

The nave and chancel of the abbey survive. The sacristy had been restored as an oratory at the brewery. The rest of what is left, including a well dedicated to St. Francis, and long held in great veneration, lie beneath the modern buildings. As the site is developed on the departure of the brewery operation, the ground will reveal its story.

A Few Kilkenny Pubs

Egan's, John St.

The Left Bank, The Parade

The Dylan, John St.

Brewery Corner, Parliament St.

Bollard's, Kieran St.

The Pumphouse, Parliament St.

Cleere's, Parliament St.

Bridie's, John St.

Rafter Dempsey's, Friary St.

Phelans, Parliament St.

O'Riada's, Parliament St.

Syd Harkin's, Rose Inn St.

Ryan's, Friary St.

The Black Abbey

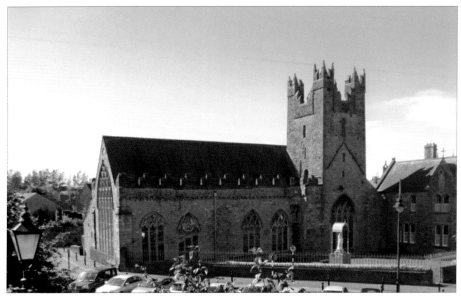

The Black Abbey is a medieval church founded by William Marshall the Younger for the Dominican Friars in 1225. It also known as the Convent of the One and Undivided Trinity.

The abbey was built outside the town walls and the nearest town gate, which still stands, is in Abbey St. and gave access to the medieval Hightown. The gate is called the Black Freren Gate, after the Black Friars.

The high wall to the left of the car park opposite the church is part of the original town walls. Being outside the walls, the Abbey also had defensive walls, now gone.

In 1990, work on the adjacent public car park uncovered 250 skeletons from the part of the medieval graveyard that was there and forgotten. The courtyard of the abbey itself contains 10 stone tombs of more of the dead from the 13th and 14th century. These are now empty.

The name Black Abbey was derived from the black cloak worn by the Dominicans ("Black Friars") over their white habits. Originally built in a typical Dominican style, little now remains of the early church except the lower part of an ancient tower (which predates the church), and

the old nave. It is the only original Dominican foundation in Ireland still in use after nearly 800 years.

It was suppressed in 1543, and eventually converted into a courthouse. It remained so until the end of the 17th century after which it fell into ruin.

Fortunately, the Dominicans took it over again in 1816, restored the nave and transept, and the church services started again.

The exterior bears the marks of the church being much larger with long-disappeared aisles. The current church is "L" shaped, suggesting it lost a transept at some stage.

The interior is very atmospheric and the sun through the stained glass windows on a sunny day paints the grey stone walled interior with a fractured rainbow of colour.

The windows by the nave are clear glazed, and the modern glass behind the altar jars slightly. The stonework throughout is excellent and the interior has a fine wooden roof.

The windows in the remaining transept have stained glass in most, depicting biblical figures and saints. The great south Rosary Window, with the intact medieval tracery of the magnificent stonework, dominates the end wall and the view of the church from the street outside.

The stained glass panels represent the Fifteen Mysteries of the Holy Rosary. The work covers almost 45 sq. m (484 sq. ft.) and was created in 1892 by Mayers of Munich.

To the right of this in an alcove is an alabaster sculpture of the Most Holy Trinity, to whom the Abbey is dedicated.

It represents God the Father enthroned, holding a crucifix with a figure of the Son, and on the crucifix is perched a dove representing the Holy Spirit. It has date of 1264 carved on it, but experts date it to around AD 1400.

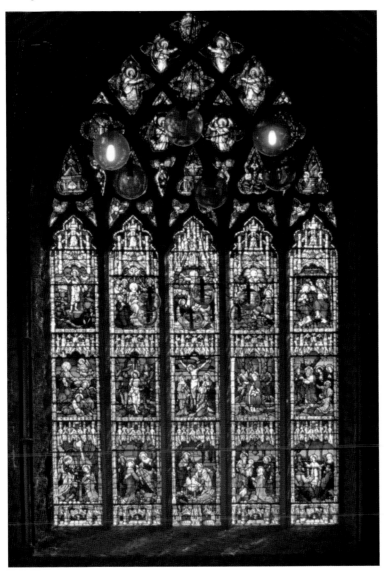

The Great Rosary window of the Black Abbey.

Watergate & Irishtown

Outside the entrance to the brewery site there is a small river running under the main road. This formed an internal dividing line in the medieval town between Hightown and Irishtown.

In the footpath by the bridge you will see marked in stone where the original town wall stood. A narrow gate would have stood across the roadway. Because of the river beneath, it was known as the Watergate. That the wall and gate was needed indicates how fraught at times the relationship was between the two communities.

Although it was joined with Hightown to form the city of Kilkenny under the Charter of 1608, Irishtown retained its own separate Corporation until 1830.

The corporation of Irishtown was made up of clerics, so it was ruled by the bishop, and the streets around the enclave still reflect the ecclesiastical history; Dean St. and Vicar St. being the two main thoroughfares.

A little further along Irishtown you come to a junction and directly across the road are St. Canice's Steps, leading to St. Canice's Cathedral.

These were built in 1641 by Robert Wale, procurator of the Cathedral, not long after Kilkenny had achieved city status under the Royal Charter.

There are a number of fragments of medieval carvings embedded in the walls after you go through the archway, which leads up to a side gate into St. Canice's churchyard.

In a small space to the right of the foot of the steps is a statue of St. Canice.

St. Canice's Steps, leading up to the cathedral.

46

15 St. Canice *(Cainneach)*

Kilkenny is an anglicisation of Cill Chainnigh, which is Gaelic for 'the church of Canice'.

To honour him, at the foot of St. Canice's Steps is his sculpted head. It is made of Kilkenny limestone, with bronze studding on the forehead.

The stone has a marble like sheen when smoothed, as the hands of his many admirers are gradually revealing.

He was born in 515 or 516, at Glengiven, in what is now County Derry and died at Aghaboe, in Co Laois, in 600.

His father was a distinguished bard who came from Waterford to Glengiven. His mother was called Maul and a church dedicated to her existed in medieval Kilkenny on the opposite side of the river from St. Canice's Cathedral.

The early years of Canice were spent watching his chieftain's flocks, but we find him in 543 at Clonard, under St. Finian. It was a class of high achievers including prominent men who became known as the Twelve Apostles of Ireland.

In 544 he was studying in the school of Glasnevin, under the tuition of St. Mobhi. He was ordained a priest in 545, and set out for Rome to obtain the blessing of Pope Vigilius.

By 550 we find him again at home in Glengiven, where he converted his foster-brother. In 565 he passed over to Scotland, where he is known as St. Kenneth but he eventually returned to Ireland.

Tradition says that he founded a monastery in Kilkenny by the round tower and cathedral which bears his name. Kilkenny was one of the last parts of Ireland to be converted to Christianity.

The story goes that in 597, Cainneach led a Christian force to Kilkenny to eliminate the last bastion of Druidic rule in Ireland.

The head of St. Canice as imagined and sculpted by Saturio Alonso in 1999. The tower of St. Canice's Cathedral can be seen in the background.

The last Archdruid of Ireland had retired with his Council to a mound in Kilkenny for safety. Cainneach led an army there and overcame them. The story is probably more fable than fact.

Aghaboe in Co Laois was the site of Cainneach's episcopal see. Under Norman influence in the twelfth century the see transferred from there to Kilkenny.

He is patron saint of the shipwrecked and Kilkenny's secondary saint after St. Kieran.

The name Canice in Old Gaelic meant 'Handsome' and remains in use in Kilkenny even to this day.

16 St. Canice's Cathedral & Round Tower

The Cathedral and its accompanying 30m high round tower are built on a steep rise and dominate the north of the city.

The Normans used grand buildings as a symbol of their strong and permanent presence and their usual practice was to build a great stone castle and a cathedral at opposite ends of the town.

In time the cathedral was a seat of power, with the bishop acting as an equal to the powers in the castle. The town walls divided the area around the cathedral (Irishtown) from Hightown.

The 13th century cathedral is the last church to be built on the site. The first was in the 6th century, long gone, and there may have been two others.

It is the original site of the Church of St. Canice after which the city and county are named. It is Ireland's second longest cathedral at 68m in length. It is the mother church of a bishopric which includes six dioceses and eight counties.

There are no records from the time of the Cathedral's construction. Studies of the building indicate that it was done in two stages.

The earliest records suggest that Bishop Hugh de Mapilton started the job around 1251 and his successor Bishop Geoffrey de St. Leger finished it by 1285.

In 1332 the central tower collapsed. Bishop Ledrede repaired the cathedral, enlarging the tower piers, reducing the tower's size, and

building up several of the adjoining arches. Most significantly, he installed a famously magnificent great East window depicting scenes from the life of Christ. Stone vaulting was added under the tower in the 1470's.

Control of the cathedral came to the Anglican Church during the Reformation instigated by Henry VIII and completed by Elizabeth I in the 16th Century.

The English Civil War (1641-1651) was a chaotic time and more so in Ireland, which was outside the theatre of war.

The Roman Catholics had the ascendancy and St. Canice's once again had a Roman Catholic bishop. This continued through the years of the 'Confederation of Kilkenny'.

This time of peaceful occupancy ended when Oliver Cromwell invaded Ireland. When he captured Kilkenny in 1650, his army damaged and devastated the Cathedral as an example to the people. The building was abandoned and roofless for twelve years.

Cardinal Rinuccini (Papal Nuncio to the Confederation of Kilkenny during the English Civil War) offered £700 for the 300 year old great East Window, installed by Bishop Ledrede, to be taken back to Rome. The then bishop turned the offer down and some years later, the window became one of the great losses of the Cromwellian occupation.

Shards of glass from the window, together with bullets made from the lead from the windows, have been found in the cathedral grounds in recent excavations.

A drawing of the windows made for Cardinal Rinuccini a few years before their destruction was used to copy the scenes from the life of Christ depicted in the originals and to reinstate the windows in 1875.

THE CATHEDRAL CLOSE.

The Close consists of the Cathedral, round tower and the various buildings and grounds in and around them. The Cathedral building we have today looks much as it did when it was first built.

The main difference is that it originally had a much higher central tower. After the first one fell, a more prudent short tower replaced it. While not as elegant, it has lasted many centuries longer than the first one. The

battlements were later adornments.

The door to the North transept has an unusual feature. On the outside, it has a circular inner arch within a pointed outer one. The rounded arch harks back to the earlier Romanesque style building used in pre-Norman times, while the pointed arch is in the Gothic style in which the cathedral is built.

As both were built at the same time, it suggests that the builder wanted some relic of the design of former churches to be reflected in the new design.

THE ROUND TOWER

The visitor's eye is drawn to the Round Tower which adjoins the Cathedral. Made from local limestone, it is the oldest surviving structure in the city of Kilkenny, It is one of the only two round towers in the country that people may climb.

Kilkenny's tower dates from the 9th century and its presence here is a sign of the antiquity of St. Canice's as an important religious site.

It is 30m (100ft) high, tapering from 4.5m to 3.3m (15ft to 11ft) in diameter. The original tower had a conical top, adding a further 5m (18ft) to its height. This is long gone.

Excavations have shown that the foundations are a mere 0.6m deep, yet the building is only 0.7m (2ft) off-plumb. To make the structure even more unstable, the excavation found the remains of two adults and two children under the foundations.

To sum up, a tower has stood here in 60 cm of foundation and set into graveyard clay. Either the builders were very smart in selecting where to build the tower or they have been very lucky.

The door to the tower is 2.7m (9 ft) off the ground and modern visitors can reach it with a convenient metal stair. When built, a wooden ladder would have been the best available.

The view from the tower on a fine day is worth the time taken making the long dark climb to the top using the 121 steps over 7 floors inside it. It will give you a new respect for the endurance and agility of the medieval monk.

The Cathedral is surrounded by a picturesque graveyard, which frames the buildings. When the restoration of the Cathedral to its present state first began in 1843, one of

The Round Tower is a feature of the Irish landscape from early medieval times. Tall, thin and needle-like, with a timber or stone cap, they were built to last, and many of them have. Almost all are built adjacent to a church or monastery. Round towers are the most significant stone buildings to have survived from pre-Norman times.

Popular belief is that these towers were primarily built to give the local community a high vantage point to watch for raiders, such as the Vikings. Once seen, the treasures and relics would be stored high off the ground. The door was high off the ground and a ladder would be pulled up afterwards, giving security to those inside.

This story has a few problems. The doors were wooden and could be set alight from a distance with a burning spear. Once lit, the tower would act like a chimney drawing smoke upwards, suffocating those inside and possibly burning the sacred books. The attackers could then enter with little resistance.

There are records of people burning to death in round towers. Even without an attack, those inside would have little space and lacking any great supply of water, could not hold out for long.

It is more likely that the original purpose of the tower was to act as a belfry. The Irish for round tower is cloigtheach, which literally translates as bellhouse. The door was built high off the ground to strengthen the structure.

Most round towers were built with very shallow foundations. To put a door at ground level would weaken the building. So a solid core was built up a few metres before the hollow structure began.

Even with this construction, most round towers are now damaged. Only two in the country can be climbed internally, St. Canice's in Kilkenny being one. There are 52 of the original round towers in the country. Many are ruins.

There are 4 more in Co. Kilkenny. Aghaviller. (page 80) , Kilree (page 81), Grangefertagh & Tullaherin.

the first jobs was to clear up the graveyard which contained the dead of over a thousand years.

The earth from so many burials had in places almost reached the windows of the Cathedral. It was tidied up, and the surplus earth banked against the wall at the back of the cathedral.

A number of the cut-stone grave markers predate 1700, and the craftsmanship is of high quality. Such gravestones are of significant importance to the region's heritage.

Other buildings around the perimeter would have been for functionaries of the Cathedral.

The Deanery is just outside the main gate. It is an 'L'-shaped detached house. The first phase was built pre-1614. The second phase was built in 1729.

The Organist's Cottage, on the left of the grounds, was built in the 17th Century. It is a three-bay single storey house with a half-dormer attic. It was originally built for the wonderfully titled Prebendary of Killamery. It was later converted into an Alms house. Now the Organist of the Cathedral and his family reside here.

Next door is the Library. It is a two storey building with six bays. It incorporates the fabric of an original grammar school and Blackrath Castle. The Cathedral library had an important theological role in the 16th Century.

The library is still preserved and protected on the second floor, which it shares with the diocesan office. Many of the books are stored elsewhere, but it still houses many important theological books. The ground floor of the library is the home of the bishop's vicar.

The bishop lived just outside the walls of the Cathedral Close in the Bishop's Palace. The earliest part of this building is from the 14th century but it has been added to over time and now looks like a Georgian residence.

It is now home of the Heritage Council, a public body set up in 1995 to help educate and develop an understanding of all parts of Irish heritage.

INSIDE THE CATHEDRAL

Built in the traditional cruciform shape of Christian churches of the time, the cathedral contains tombs of bishops, lords and ladies as well as memorials to merchants.

The south facing main porch contains memorials on either side to members of the community who lost their lives in the Great War and the Second World War. Already in decline, some of these were the last of their line and the family names are no longer part of the Kilkenny story.

Inside the doors, one experiences the sense of peace which is found in all places of worship. Guided tours of the cathedral are given throughout the day and are well worth taking.

Please remember this is a house of worship and act accordingly. There are booklets in a variety of languages to help you enjoy the features of the building.

One of the first features you meet is the baptismal Font. This is the original which has been a part of the church since it was built.

Damaged and removed by Cromwell's soldiers once their horses had finished drinking from it, it is now restored to its position by the door to welcome each new Christian into the community.

The font cover is modern – depicting the sea of life and the fish showing the traditional symbol of Christianity.

Made of timber, the roofs were also a casualty of the Cromwellian army and the current roof dates from the mid 19th century. The hammerbeam bosses were carved in 1865.

The fir roofing was not weatherproof and the many draughts were terrible in cold and windy weather. When snow fell, it was blown right in, to cover the patient congregation beneath. Even a hardy Victorian could not endure this for long, so it all had to be re-roofed in 1879.

The cathedral has a wealth of tombs and monuments, including those of bishops and lords as well as merchants and tradesmen. Again, the older ones suffered from the

Below: Nave and altar.   *Facing page: Cathedral roof and nave.*

Kilkenny by night

despoiling of the building by the Cromwellians. Some were smashed and most were overturned. As a result, when re-erected in the 19th century, there was no record of where some had originally stood and some of the tombs have panels or tops from other ones which were totally destroyed.

What is left of these early tombs is still of interest. One, from around 1600, shows a cock perched on a pot. A medieval legend told how, on the day of the Crucifixion, a cock being cooked for Judas Iscariot's dinner rose out of the pot and crowed. Realising that this foretold Christ's Resurrection, Judas returned the thirty pieces of silver and hanged himself.

Nearby there are three craftsmen's slabs, bearing the symbols of their tools and trades – carpenter, weaver and cobbler.

Carved Lion of St. Mark the Evangelist adorns the Choir Stall

In the side aisle is a model of the city of Kilkenny as it looked in 1640. A much smaller city than now, it was a few years after it had been granted its Charter from King James I and before the upheaval caused in years to come in the wake of its capture in the Cromwellian wars.

The south transept (or right 'arm' of the cross shaped church) is the burial place for the Butler family, who since the 13th century have been the Ormond Lords of Kilkenny Castle.

The centre piece is the tomb of the 8th Earl, Piers and his wife Margaret Butler, whose effigies rest, frozen in time, on the top. On the wall beside it is the monument of the 9th Earl, James, who was poisoned in London, along with 35 of his servants and retinue.

No Ormondes were buried in the cathedral for 200 years from the mid 1700's, and the family vaults were covered over and lost to memory.

The present vault was built in 1854 on the death of the then Marquis. Just 10 years later, while the old classical choir was being stripped, the original vaults were found either side of the altar and under the present organ. The bodies from them were re-interred in the new vault and the old one sealed and covered over again.

Nearby, on display, is one of the seven volumes of the Great War Memorial List which records names of Irishmen who fell in the Great European War 1914-1918. The committee compiled the seven volumes of the Irish National War memorial with decorative borders by Harry Clarke.

The north transept contains the slab of the Kyteler family tomb, which was found under the High Street pavement in 1894. It also contains an ancient stone seat known as St. Kieran's chair.

The stone under the seat is said to have been part of the original bishop's throne at Aghaboe (c. 400), where the original cathedral was, and brought here when the church on this spot became the cathedral. The sides are about the same age as the cathedral, and thus are probably from the original clergy stalls or seats in the choir. The bishop is enthroned here.

The choir stalls, before the main altar, are made of Danubian oak, hand-carved at Bruges, Belgium in 1899 and based on the Bruges cathedral stalls of 1470. End panels depict scenes from the history of the cathedral.

The floor of the sanctuary, on which the altar stands, contain a symbolic depiction of reconciliation between the Christian traditions in Ireland.

There are four marbles used in the floor and each represents a province from where the stone came. Green Connemara marble is for Connacht, black Kilkenny marble for Leinster, red marble from Cork for Munster and grey marble from Tyrone for Ulster. The floors are the work of the architect Richard Langrishe.

To the left of the sanctuary, in a niche in the wall, is the tomb of Bishop Richard Ledrede, infamous for one of Europe's earliest witch burnings in the case against Alice Kyteler. (see page 117)

To the left of the great doors at the other end of the nave is the tomb of Bishop John Kearney, who died in 1813.

Genealogists have identified him as a great-great-great grand uncle of former US President, Barak Obama. The Bishop still has direct descendants living in the county today.

Open:
May to Sept: Mon - Sat. 9.00 - 18.00.
Sun 14.00 - 18:00.
Oct - Apr. : Mon - Sat. 10.00 - 17.00.
Sun Closed
Round Tower opens at 10am.
Admission fee applies.
Tel: 056 776 4971
www.stcanicescathedral.com

Please remember this is a house of worship. Dress and act appropriately.

John St.

At the end of Rose Inn St., Johns Bridge crosses the River Nore.

Before crossing the bridge to your right is Canal Square which is the start of a 2km walk between the river and the castle grounds along a tree shaded pathway which attracts runners, walkers and strollers throughout the year.

There was an actual canal down here. It was the small beginnings of a project in the 19th century which failed for lack of money, but it adds to the picturesque river views and restful background.

Tynans Bridge House Bar - a step back in time

Today the square holds a large limestone statue to Kilkenny's hurlers.

It is 4m tall and weighs 2 tonnes. The sculptor started with a 20 tonne block of stone and it took three years to produce the final piece.

On your left before crossing is Tynans Bridge House Bar. This is a an original Victorian Bar and held in almost the same esteem with the locals as the venerable churches and national monuments which fill the city.

The middle of the bridge is a good viewing point for the Castle. Facing up river you see the Lady Desart footbridge.

Once you cross the river, John St. lies before you. From here up to St. Johns Priory and about 100m on either side was the medieval suburb of St. Johns.

A separate walled enclave, little of the original buildings or walls survive and the street is mainly given over to pubs and restaurants, which are one of the attractions of the modern city.

The Pride of Kilkenny by Brian Wrafter. Kilkenny's monumental hurlers.

17 Butler Gallery

Photo: Danny Mulligan

In 1943, a group of farseeing Kilkenny people decided to create an art society to showcase the work of Irish artists and also to exhibit major international artists.

Its first home was in a local Technical school and the society struggled. However, in the 1960s a new interest in Art arose and the Society found a home in the basement of Kilkenny Castle.

During its existence, the Society gave Kilkenny people an opportunity to experience and enjoy works in a variety of media while at the same time the Gallery gathered together a collection of works from Irish and international artists, many who have since become major figures in their fields.

In 2020, the Gallery moved to a new home, a 10,000 sq ft building on John's Quay. It has seven exhibition galleries.

The Gallery collection owns works by Irish artists Paul Henry, Louis LeBroquy, Manie Jellett and Mary Swanzy.

The highlight of the collection is that of the works of local artist Tony O'Malley (see page 119), whose wife donated a large body of his work for display in the Gallery.

Since its foundation, the Gallery has give free access to its exhibitions and this continues to be the case since it moved to its new home.

The building that is home to the Butler Gallery was formerly an almshouse built on the site of the city's original military barracks.

Joseph Evans, a local philanthropist bequeathed his fortune to built a school, to provide support for orphans, apprenticeships and marriage dowries for the poor and £5,000 to set up an almshouse to support ten men and ten women from among the 'deserving' poor. It became know as Evans' Home.

The almshouse continued to serve its function for almost 170 years. Income from the trust that Evans set up lasted from its start in 1818 to the mid-1990s.

One stipulation was that those living there would never be asked to pay any rent. Thus when inflation eventually exhausted the Trust's funds, there was nothing left to support the work of the almshouse in caring for its residents.

The local library service used the building but without funds to maintain and modernise the it, the Home fell into disuse. Since then the Kilkenny local authority took it over and imaginatively repurposed it as an art gallery for the public. Surely Joseph Evans would approve.

18 Great War Memorial

KILKENNY WORLD WAR I MEMORIAL 1914-1918

In 1914, the world descended into a war which lasted four long years and changed society forever.

At the time, Ireland was still part of the United Kingdom, ruled directly fro London. Many people in Ireland had been pushing for a form of self rule, the Home Rule movement, with a satellite government in Dublin as the goal for many.

This was seen by many staunch Unionists in Ulster as being unacceptable and they armed themselves to resist it, forming the Ulster Volunteers in 1912.

Seeing an armed threat from Ulster, many in the rest of Ireland formed the National Volunteers and a Company was formed in Kilkenny in 1914.

While the tensions grew on both sides, larger forces intervened and the invasion of Belgium by Germany on August 3rd 1914 lead to an outbreak of war. An appeal was made by the British Government for volunteers to fight in France.

Many in both the Ulster and National Volunteers enlisted.. A small number of National Volunteers did not and remained at home to pursue a new vision; that of Irish independence.

Enlistment to fight in the army was a personal decision. Conscription did not apply in Ireland. Some idealists did so to protect small nations such as Belgium from annihilation. Others joined because a soldiers pay was regular and more than they already earned. A few patriotically did it for King and Country.

Over 3,000 people from Kilkenny city and county left to fight in the war. More than 800 of these never returned home.

Those that did came home to a changed country, heading into an armed war on independence against the Government from which they had fought for over the previous four years.

For a century, the experiences and sacrifices of those who left were deliberately forgotten. It took Ireland almost a century to acknowledge their legacy.

A voluntary group set out to remember those forgotten local men and women and in 2018 they saw the fruits of years of work with the unveiling of a memorial to those who died in the Great War.

There are 828 name son the wall. Five are women and 324 of those named have no known grave. The youngest was 14 years old.

The memorial is located on the bank of the river Nore 100m from the Butler Gallery and can be seen from the Lady Desart bridge.

19 St. John's Church

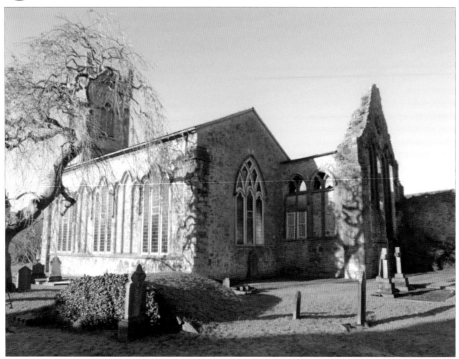

Church of St. John the Evangelist in the winter time.
The roofless part to the right is the remains of the medieval church which stood in the site.

The Priory of St. John occupied its own enclave on the east side of the River Nore from the 13th century. The outline of the precinct can be seen on the map on page 65.

It was founded by the monks of the Canons Regular of St. Augustine, the Augustinians. The monks provided an unusual service in addition to the spiritual side of their ministry.

They provided accommodation for trainee knights, particularly to the Knights Hospitaller of St. John of Jerusalem. Outside the walls were jousting areas and combat arenas. Inside the walls were the living quarters for the trainees and their servants.

One area of the city, near St. Canice's Cathedral, is called the Butts, a memory of the time when the area was used for archery practice. The shooting arena in archery is known as the butts.

The Knights Hospitaller were a religious and military order, originally set up as a monastic order to found a hospital in Jerusalem for pilgrims.

As unrest in the Holy Land resulted from the First and subsequent Crusades, the order started to provide armed escorts for travellers and before long it had become an order of men in chain mail mounted on chargers.

Before joining the order, applicants had to learn to fight. Kilkenny was home to one of their schools.

In time the order faded and the Augustinians lost income. They started to sell plots of land inside the walls to ordinary citizens.

This piecemeal sell off resulted in the dismantling of the buildings to build many new homes and businesses in their place.

By the time that Henry VIII dissolved the

priory in the 16th century, only a church and some adjacent buildings were left.

At the time of the Confederation, when the city was under Catholic rule, the Jesuits briefly gained control of the building but the arrival of Oliver Cromwell with his troops five years later saw them quickly scattered.

The main remaining piece today is St. John's church, at the junction of John Street and Michael Street.

Over the years the building fell into ruins, but in 1817 the Lady Chapel was re-roofed and converted into a parish church to serve the Church of Ireland parish of St. John.

Part of the original Lady Chapel has been integrated into the 19th century building. St. John's was once known as the Lantern of Ireland due to the effect created by the candles from the church illuminating the surrounding area through its fine windows.

The few sightless windows now look on to a quiet graveyard and a busy street nearby.

The church is used weekly for public worship and may be open to the public in the summer months.

Maudlin St. Tower

Just beyond St. John's church and to the right lies Maudlin St. The name is a corruption of Magdalene. The right hand side of the street is built along the line of the original wall around St. John's precinct.

About 100m along the road is the Bastion, a small tower which marked the corner of the wall. It is sadly much reduced from its original state.

From here you can look back to the corner of the priory site which will give you a good idea

Many diseases in medieval times were confused with leprosy, including psoriasis, impetigo and syphilis.

Leper hospitals were also called lazar houses, after the man in the parable of Lazarus and Dives, who was described as a beggar covered in sores, sitting at a rich man's gate.

Popular belief was that the Lazarus who was raised from the dead by Jesus, was also a leper.

A further misbelief was that Mary, Sister of Lazarus, was also Mary Magdalene. As the second Mary was believed to have been a loose woman, which was unclean and associated with leprosy, the medieval mind dedicated leper hospitals to Mary Magdalene.

As lepers were felt to be suffering the punishments of Purgatory on earth, they had an early passport to Paradise, and be able to intervene on behalf of this whose charity had sustained them in life. This charity paid for the running of the hospitals.

of how small the medieval settlement really was.

A further 150m along brings you to the Maudlin St. Tower. Built in 1327, its original purpose was as a hospital for lepers and dedicated to St. Mary Magdalene. In medieval times, lepers were not allowed into the crowded streets of towns or cities and, as in this case, their hospital is built outside the town wall.

The Augustinians would have managed the hospital. In time, the hardship of life at the time, which included the Black Death joining the usual plagues, pestilence and famine, killed off the weak, which included the lepers.

Kilkenny was left with a fine hospital and the opportunity to make money from it was not lost. In a change of direction, it now worked to cure the wealthy, which was much more profitable.

We know this because excavations of the ground around showed bones from the meals at the time which were beef, mutton and fowl. Food that the rich could afford.

Although the hospital is beside a river, fish does not appear to have been popular. The patients also had access to the hospital garden and orchards.

Like everything else, when the dissolution of the church occurred, the hospital, which was run by the monks, closed.

There is no public access to the tower.

21 Macdonagh Junction Famine Monument

MacDonagh Junction Shopping Centre at the top of John St. is built on the site of the old Kilkenny Union Workhouse.

Workhouses were built across Ireland in the 1830's after the passing of the Poor Laws which were to deal with the misery of poverty suffered by many in Ireland and England at that time.

130 workhouses were built in Ireland and the building in Kilkenny started in 1840 and was finished in 1842, in time for Ireland's greatest calamity of the last millennium, the Great Famine.

Life in the workhouse was not easy for the poor. By law, those unlucky enough to need to move to a workhouse were provided with food, clothing and accommodation purposely worse in standard than the ordinary worker. For this they had to work hard for no pay.

This system was designed to deter the poor, whose

Thomas Macdonagh (Irish: Tomás Mac Donnchadha; 1878 – 1916) was an Irish political activist, poet, playwright, educationalist and volunteer soldier. He was founder of the ASTI, the secondary school teachers' association.

He is best known as one of the leaders of the Easter Rising of 1916, as the Commander of the Dublin Brigade of the Irish Volunteers and as a signatory of the Proclamation of Independence of the Irish Republic. He was one of those executed for his part in this.

Macdonagh taught at St. Kieran's College in Kilkenny in his early career and while here became deeply involved in the Gaelic League, which had its local headquarters in Rothe House. It was here that he taught Irish for a time, before moving to Dublin to fulfil his wish for Irish freedom and destiny for martyrdom.

Reproduced by kind permission of An Post ©

later, after the country side was ravaged with Famine, there were 4,000 souls living there dependant on the meagre charity. Kilkenny was far from being the worst hit part of the country.

During the height of the famine years of 1846 and 1847, almost 1,350 people died in the Kilkenny workhouse. There would have been many more in the greater community. The cemeteries could not handle the number of bodies to be buried and the workhouse opened a communal grave in its own grounds.

This grave was rediscovered during the building of MacDonagh Junction and 975 bodies were found. These have now been reburied on the site and a small monument to so many lost lives marks their final resting place.

In 1872, the Sisters of Mercy took over the running of the workhouse and conditions eased. The workhouse system ended in Ireland in 1923, when the Kilkenny one closed.

Kilkenny's railway station opened in 1851, adjacent to the workhouse. It was renamed after the 1916 rebel leader, Thomas MacDonagh. The workhouse site is now part of the MacDonagh Junction shopping centre.

Recognising its heritage, the Shopping Centre provides a free audio-visual tour of the site. While much of the miserable conditions no longer exist, the story s powerfully delivered and ends with the story of John and Patrick Saul from Dublin who, having been abandoned by their parents in Dublin, tried to walk to Clonmel but ended up in the Kilkenny Union Workhouse.

Fittingly, a statue of two boys playing and climbing, as young boys will, marks the end of the tour and is located in the Famine Memorial Garden beside the final resting place of the last remains of the 975 inmates found on the site.

condition was thought to result from their own lazy ways, from seeking an easy life. Families were pulled apart in a system of strict segregation, to add to the misery of their state.

A workhouse was set up in each Union. There was a Union and a workhouse, in Callan, Thomastown and Urlingford as well as Kilkenny. The latter was one of the largest in the country at the time. Other Unions covered the south of the county and Waterford.

In 1838, when the Poor Laws were passed, Co Kilkenny had almost 200,000 inhabitants. To put this in perspective, the county of Kilkenny has a current population of less than 90,000. Pre-Famine Ireland was a very crowded land.

When it opened in 1842, the Kilkenny Workhouse had 760 inmates. Less than a decade

Kilkenny Famine Experience is a free audio-visual tour that tells the stories of those who lived and died within the workhouse walls.
Tours each morning and afternoon Mon. - Fri.
Afternoons only on weekend and Bank Holidays. Enquiries at the Customer Service desk.
www.kilkennyfamineexperience.com
Tel: 056-7777600

22 The City Walls & Talbot's Tower

The Medieval town of Hightown in Kilkenny was a rectangle approx 800m x 350m. Its perimeter was approx 1.45 km and enclosed about 28ha. It was bounded to the north by the Breagagh River, which is crossed today on the way to St. Canice's cathedral, and on the east by the River Nore. This left the rest of the town undefended, a dangerous state of affairs in 13th century Ireland.

The Anglo Norman saw the defensive benefits of a town wall as well as the opportunities it gave to collect tolls and taxes and to keep watch on visitors coming and going. In addition, walls gave status and created a sense of identity for those who lived inside.

Murage grants were obtained from the crown, allowing the levying of tolls, and the construction started in the mid 13th century. On the north side, the wall was bounded and protected by the River Bregagh. No stone walls were built facing the river Nore, although wooden walls may have existed. Stone walls were built on the western and southern sides of the city in time.

Walls were also built to protect Irishtown and St. John's. The first encircled an area around St. Canice's cathedral to the river Nore, to the north of Hightown. This was approx 10ha in size. Part of the wall still exists as a boundary to the north side of the cathedral close.

The second was St. John's across the Nore, which was 4.5 ha in size. A small circular open-backed tower on Maudlin Street represents the most accessible remainder of this wall and would have acted as a flanking tower for musket shot on the north-east wall.

Four towers and a bastion defended the western wall. Talbot's Tower on the south west corner is the most significant surviving part of the defences. It can be seen from the Ormonde Road and the car park of Ormonde College. It is currently under renovation. It was almost 10m high, 5.5m in diameter with walls 1.6m thick.

The southern stretch of wall ran from Talbot's Tower to Kilkenny Castle which anchored the approach from the seaward side up the river.

Talbot's Tower. Part of the remaining town defences.

There were six gates, Black Freren gate in Abbey St. (next page) being the last one left to us today. Some of the remainder are remembered in names such as Watergate, which was the internal gate between Hightown and Irishtown. The nearby theatre in Parliament St, still keeps the name alive.

The ultimate test came in 1650, when the forces of Oliver Cromwell laid siege to the city. The walls withstood bombardment but were initially breached through a gate in Irishtown and later, after the fall of the suburb of St. John's, the gate at the river, where John's bridge now stands, came under attack.

When it became obvious that the defenders could no longer hold out, due to debilitation from plague, the population surrendered before the walls finally crumbled.

Remnants of the wall still exist with some parts reaching to 4.5m in height. In parts, where the modern street crosses where the original wall stood, there are limestone flags in set in the footpath showing where this happens.

These can be seen in Friary St., just past the Capuchin Friary, and at the entrance to Irishtown, at the Watergate bridge.

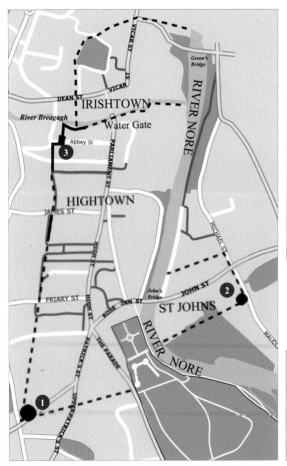

In 1420, Henry V issued a murage grant which allowed the town of Kilkenny to apply tolls on certain goods brought into the town. The money collected was to be used to build the walls.

Alongside tolls on grain, timber, fish, meat, nails, fleeces, wine and honey, the king allowed a toll of 1/2d be levied on every 100 skins of cat brought in to be sold.

So ironically, since Kilkenny people are known as Kilkenny Cats, the defence of the town was paid for in part by a tax on the skins of cats.

- - - - ▶ Route of the City Walls
───── Remaining City Wall
1 Talbot's Tower
2 Maudlin St. Bastion
3 Black Freren Gate

The Black Abbey seen through Black Freren Gate in Abbey St. This was one of the smallest gates to the city and used by the Dominican monks who owned the abbey and lands outside the gate. They had a key which gave access to the city from their own walled enclave around the abbey. Called the Black friars after the black robes they wore, the gate is named after them.

Kilkenny
County

Unlike the wild countryside of the Western seaboard, land in Kilkenny has been tamed by a thousand years of cultivation. Not for the Normans the shared land usage of the Irish clan, held nominally by the local king but in reality by strength of arms. Celtic ownership was recorded in the songs of the bards and the poetry of the filí (poets). It was marked with ogham stones.

The Normans brought title deeds, leases, clerks and fences to mark out what was theirs, taken from the Irish natives who lacked documents to show ownership. Lands were cleared in this part of the country, while much of Ireland was still forested. Sheep cropped the hillsides and fields were ploughed for grain crops.

Through the centuries, land was reclaimed, drained, fertilised and maintained. In time, grand estates appeared where manicured lawns and formal gardens were accompanied by swards of pasture. So don't expect to see wild untamed nature. It is there but buried in a landscape shaped by man, from the Knockroe passage tomb to the formal gardens of Woodstock House.

The following chapter takes you through the towns of the county, from a market town like Callan to a picture postcard village such as Inistioge.

Rather than take you on a prescribed route, it leaves you choose your own way, to ramble from place to place following your inclination and your interests. There is also background on Anglo-Norman Tower houses and Celtic Crosses, which you will find on your travels.

You can mix your trip with visits to craft workshops, country walks or activities which can add an extra dimension to your experience.

Kilkenny County is best visited by car, although some cycling trails are being developed. With the city to the north of the county, much of what you will see is to the south. It is easy to lose yourself in the windy country roads which seem to travel on forever through rolling countryside.

A number of the sites are accessed through private land. Please respect the owners rights and observe the countryside code.
1. Be safe - plan ahead and follow any signs
2. Leave gates and property as you find them
3. Protect plants and animals, and take your litter home
4. Keep dogs under close control
5. Consider other people

Previous page: Bridge over River Nore at Inistioge

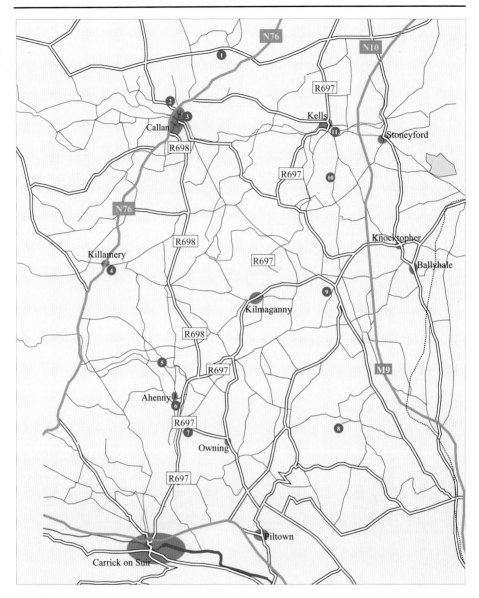

1. Spirit of Place - James Hoban
2. Augustinian Abbey - Callan
3. Westcourt - Callan
4. Killamery High Cross
5. Knockroe Passage Grave
6. Ahenny High Crosses

7. Kilkieran High Crosses
8. Kilmogue Dolmen
9. Aghaviller & Castlemorris Estate
10. Kilree High Cross & Tower
11. Kells Priory

Spirit of Place

James Hoban, the architect who designed the White House in Washington, was born in Desart, Cuffesgrange.

"Spirit of Place", a national memorial to his memory, is near, but not exactly where, the Hoban home was. The house still stood until the 1940s.

The memorial consists of a small arbour and a structure designed and built in 2008 by twenty four students from the Catholic University of Washington.

The structure is 30 metres long and as high as 3 metres, incorporating almost all local stone but with some Italian marble, and glass panels shooting up into space.

The thought behind it is to mirror the uplifting character of Hoban's struggles and triumphs, his migration from low ground to the high ground of the New World of democracy in America.

On entering it, the first section is made of rubble and rough stone, like the stone walls built between fields, early technology. The second section features more refined, cut stone to reflect emotions that were more refined. The third is made of Kilkenny limestone, ending with Italian marble which, like the White House, is more pure and polished.

The structure also incorporates glass panels on which are etched words such as 'perseverance', 'struggle', 'triumph' and 'rising', in English and in Irish, reflecting of the bond between Irish and American culture and history.

Impressive and modern, it is far from the architecture of Hoban but as an imaginative architect he would probably prefer to be remembered as a modern man.

Read Hoban's story on page 116.

To get there: Midway between Kilkenny and Callan on the N76, turn off for Cashel & Killenaule. The memorial is 1.5km along this road on the left. There is a small parking area.

Spirit of Place. The national James Hoban memorial

Callan *(Callain)*

Located 15 km south west of Kilkenny city lies the market town of Callan. It reputedly gets its name from the High King of Ireland, Niall Caille.

The story is that, in a war with the Vikings, the High King arrived in Callan to find that its river was in flood. He saw his servant trying to cross the river and being swept away by the fast flowing current.

King Niall is recorded in history as a man of action. Seeing the impending disaster, he unwisely urged his horse into the fast flowing river to try to save his servant, only to be also overcome and drowned by the flood.

In memory of his rash deed, the river on which Callan is built is named the "Kings River".He is buried at Kilree near the round tower. (see page 81)

When the Normans arrived, they first built a massive motte and bailey castle by the river. The motte still stands and can be seen from the main road bypassing the town. The property can be visited but is little more than a gigantic man made earthen mound, covered by trees.

The town was founded by William Marshall in the 13th century and over time walls were built to protect it as wealth grew. It was an important town for the Ormond Butlers and was prominent enough to have two MPs in the Irish House of Commons.

Its wealth and prominence made it a target for Cromwell's army in 1650. The besieged town people put up a fierce resistance but the town Governor surrendered the main castle without firing a shot.

The town was sacked, the inhabitants slaughtered and the area left in ruins. Times were tough for the town. Callan people however always hoped for a better day. One rhyme which all Callan people cling to states.

"Kells was, Kilkenny is and Callan will be, the greatest of the three."

Unwilling to wait for Callan's time to come, some of Callan's children have gone out to the world to change it.

In addition to James Hoban on the previous page, Callan is also the birthplace of Blessed Edmund Ignatius Rice, artist Tony O'Malley and playwright Tom Kilroy.

Their stories are found later in this book.

② Augustinian Abbey

This is a former Augustinian friary in an area on the north-east of the town known as Abbey Meadow and is a magnificent ruin of a building.

In peaceful isolation, its mullioned windows and grey tower link Callan with a period of devastating change in the history of Ireland, the Dissolution of the monasteries by Henry VIII.

At the beginning, a local gentleman requested permission from Pope Pius II to build a friary but it was his son who eventually built it in 1467, as part of a settlement under which he received a dispensation to marry a relative.

It soon became an observant community adopting the strict monastic rules then in vogue in Europe. The Augustinians had come to Ireland in the late thirteenth century and Ireland was part of the English Province of the order. For a long time, all the friars were English.

By the time that Callan was built, the Irish province had been formed and an Augustinian professor of theology was based in St. Patrick's in Dublin.

The Order grew in the coming centuries until its world changed when Henry VIII decided to establish an English Church and

suppressed all the existing catholic religious houses. The Earls of Ormond took over the lands at this time.

The Augustinians were not giving up and a new monastery was built in Callan in 1766. It is in Mill St. but no longer has any friars in residence.

The old friary church is a long, rectangular building with a central bell-tower. The east end or choir, is lit by a fine east window and in its south wall is a fine sedelia (a seat for officiating priests).

The domestic buildings and the cloister court no longer survive. However, a freshwater well still remains on the grounds of the abbey.

 # Westcourt

Blessed Edmund Ignatius Rice was born at Westcourt in Callan. He was fortunate in that his parents were not poor and his family were tenant farmers with 200 acres.

The house was large for its time with four bedrooms and, though built in 1680, has remained relatively unchanged since then.

While Edmund travelled to Waterford in his late teens to form a life of his own, his brother and step sisters remained in the Callan area. In later years when he needed a safe environment for his only daughter to grow up in, Edmund brought her back to his family home.

The home at Westcourt remained with descendants of the Rice family until the 1960s when the Christian Brothers bought it with four acres.

The home has been restored and is now a museum which is open to visitors and guided tours are available. Tour groups of 50 to 60 people are not uncommon.

A church was built beside it, as well as a visitors centre and Westcourt has fittingly become a place of prayer pilgrimage as well as heritage.

Read his story on page 120.

The thatched cottage where Edmund Rice was born and raised, now open for all to visit.

Callan Workhouse & the Famine Graveyard

Callan workhouse opened for business in 1841 and served a hinterland of 42,700 people. Managing the workhouse were a Master, matron, clerk chaplain, schoolmaster, porter.

It cost £5,500 to build and a further £1,120 to fit out. Situated at the south end of the town, the grounds covered over 6 acres. It was built to accommodate 600 people.

In its first years of operation, the Callan Workhouse functioned very well, but the Great Famine which started in 1845 was too great for the operation and it became near unmanageable.

At the height of the Famine, many thousands were looking for relief there. Even after the Famine, in 1851 it had over 2,100 residents.

Between 1841 and 1851 a total of 1,411 people, 688 males and 723 females, died in Callan Workhouse, a further 2,104, 1,050 males and 1,054 females died in the temporary fever sheds.

Thus over 3,500 people died her in the five years from 1846 to 1850.

This was not as severe as parts of the West and South West of the country but still shocking.

After the famine years, the workhouse settled back to the level of operation for which it was built.

It stayed in operation until the 1920s. In 1922 it was garrisoned by Free State troops during the Civil War and was later sold to private individuals and public bodies. It now partly houses some local authority sections.

There is a small memorial plaque in Canon Kennedy Court, adjacent to the remaining buildings which shows two pages from the workhouse register showing admittances and discharges. The pages puts the misery and sadness of the times down in neat figures and columns.

The workhouse can be found behind of the Fire Station at the top of Green St.

The poor of the workhouse, who had no family to bury them, were buried in a 'paupers' grave in the Famine Graveyard at Cherryfield.

It is located in a remote one and a quarter acre site outside of the town. Continue south on Green St., past the water tower, parallel to the main road, crossing the Windgap/Clonmel road, for one mile. Just after crossing a bridge, the turning for the graveyard is to your left. You need to walk from here.

Because cherries grew there in times gone by it is still popularly known as Cherryfield.

Most of those buried in here were victims of the Great Famine which devastated Ireland during the 1840s.

Originally it was intended to have the graveyard closer to the town, but it was cheaper to buy a site in this area of poorer common land.

Stories have passed down about the endless procession of funerals from the Workhouse, or Poorhouse as it was generally called, and the misery and degradation that surrounded them.

It is said that often up to six bodies at a time were carted out for burial, and that it was not uncommon for corpses to fall off the 'funeral cart' because the boreen into Cherryfield was so rough and muddy.

Indeed the current path gives an idea of what the full road taken by the funeral must have been like.

The graveyard was roughly fenced off at the time and was fully enclosed by a wall in the 1860s, with a substantial gate and entry piers. Cherryfield continued as a 'pauper graveyard' up until the closing down of the workhouse.

The graveyard has little of how we would regard a final resting place of the dead. The poor could not afford headstones and all were buried in unmarked graves. The peaceful scene of today gives little of the feeling of desperation and despair which it must have had in the height of the Famine years of the nineteenth century.

Ossory High Crosses

Early Celtic Christians created the high cross as a visible sign of their faith. They were raised primarily during the Early Middle Ages. Celtic crosses are free standing, are often richly decorated and frequently feature a stone ring around the intersection.

They reproduce in stone patterns developed in earlier wooden crosses, complete with designs which mimic the metalwork that held the wooden cross together.

While later high crosses concentrated on scenes from the bible, these earlier crosses carried intricate interlace designs on almost every surface and only the bases tend to have and carved figures.

Early crosses were made in the 7th century and some of the country's finest examples of early crosses are part of what is known as the West Ossory Group.

Three of these sites are west and south of Callan. They and are at Ahenny, Kilkieran and Killamery. A fourth, Kilree is near the monastic settlement of Kells. Ahenny stands as the finest of the group.

Some of these ancient monuments are in the middle of fields that form part of working farms. Please respect this and close gates behind you and do not litter where you go.

4 Killamery High Cross

8km from Callan on the main road to Clonmel (N76) is the small hamlet of Killamery. There is a signpost by the car park at the junction for the Killamery High Cross, which is 300 meters up the road.

Sited in an old graveyard, the cross is 3.65 metres high. It is known as the Snake-Dragon cross. Most of the figure sculpture is on it west face. The east face shows three marigold designs on the shaft. The boss in the centre of the head is surrounded by intertwining serpents with an open mouthed dragon above the boss. The cross has a cap-stone and the narrow sides have double mouldings.

At the end of the southern arm is a panel depicting Noah in the Ark. The end of the northern arm shows four scenes centred around John the Baptist.

There is also a worn inscription on the base of the western side of the cross which is said to read as 'OR DO MAELSECHNAILL' a prayer for Maelsechnaill. Maelsechnaill was the High King of Ireland from 846 to 862.

The western face has a Sun Swastika at the centre and has figure sculpture around the whorl, to the left is a hunting scene and to the right a chariot scene. Above the whorl is scene showing a figure holding a baby with another figure to the right of them. Below the sun disc is a crucifixion scene. The shaft of this face bears two ornate panels. Above is a fret pattern and below is a key pattern.

South face of Killamery High Cross

5 Knockroe Passage Grave

On the fringe of the border with Co Tipperary in the South West of the county lies the passage tomb of Knockroe.

Predating the Pyramids of Egypt and Stonehenge, in style and purpose, it is a grandparent of the younger Newgrange and Knowth tombs in Co Meath. And yet only in recent years has any intense investigation of the site begun.

An early place of pagan worship, it still sees modern day druids on special days such as the winter solstice, continuing a tradition of worship, carried on for millennia.

The Knockroe site was not just randomly selected. There is no doubt that this location was chosen for very specific reasons based on the landscape around it.

It is one of a group of burial mounds aligned with a large mound on Sliabhnamon in Co Tipperary 15 km away.

Don't be put off by the initial appearance of the site. Looking like a random group of stones in a fenced of part of a farmers field, these are the remains of two neolithic passage tombs.

When new, they would probably have been covered by an earthen mound, with the stones forming passages within the man made hill.

The earthen blanket has long since gone, leaving a skeleton of standing stones. Quartz is scattered around the site and these may have been used to decorate parts of the original mound, such as entrances.

Known locally as 'The Caiseal', it has two passages on the southern side. The passage to the east has a cruciform chamber with a sill stone towards the front with very large kerbstones where the southern side loops around to the western passage.

Although the western passage has a more simple design it is more interesting in that it has an alignment to the winter solstice and on both sides of the entrance are several large graded orthostats (large rocks) that give the impression of a court when viewed from the front.

Unlike the more famous Newgrange which works on dawn light, the roof-box in Knockroe's western tomb allows the rays of the setting sun to pass along the upward-sloping passage on 21st December, when it illuminates a tall red-sandstone portal.

Ancient Celtic whorls and designs, now weathered after 5,000 years.

What makes Knockroe very special is the number of Celtic symbols chiseled onto the huge stones which, though weather worn, are still visible today almost 5,000 years after they were first carved.

There are 30 stones with carvings here, more than any Irish site outside of the Boyne valley group. The artwork shows similarity with decorations found in tombs from the same time in Brittany.

Several of the stones are decorated with megalithic art similar to the later tombs at Newgrange in the Boyne Valley. The carvings need to be seen in good light as years of erosion have reduced their definition.

To get to Knockroe from Callan take the R697 south to Carrick on Suir for 15km. A small road is at your right, and a sign post opposite is for Knockroe and the Slate Quarries. Coming north from Carrick on Suir, take the same road north for 9km to the same junction.

Travel up this road, which wobbles over and back across the county border, for 1.5km passing the picturesque Slate Quarries, until coming to a T junction. Turn right and travel another few hundred meters until you see a sign to the site.

6 Ahenny High Crosses

Ahenny is just over the county border in Co Tipperary and is a small village of terraced workmen's cottages.

There are two highly decorated crosses here and they date from the 8th or 9th century, making them amongst the earliest of the ringed high crosses.

The North cross is taller at 3.65 meters. As with many remnants of past ages that have been exposed to the weather for over 1,200 years, much detail has been worn down. Because of this, the best time to view them is around mid-day during the summer, when the high relief of the sculpture is shown at its best. Both feature typical interlacing and design on the arms and cross pieces.

The taller North cross features a removable cap stones known as a mitre (bishop's hat).

The panels on the base can be difficult to make out. The north face is said to carry scenes of a procession with a chariot. The south face shows a funeral procession with a cleric holding a processional cross followed by a horse bearing a headless body which is being attacked by ravens and a man carrying the head. This may be David returning in triumph with the head of Goliath. Adam is naming the animals on the east face and the mission of the apostles and/or the Seven Bishops appears on the west face.

The smaller cross is more weather worn and the scenes on its base are almost beyond recognition. It is said to depict hunting scenes on the north face, Daniel in the Lion's Den on the east face and The Fall of Man on the south face.

A local legend is that a headache sufferer can get relief by placing one of the stone caps from the crosses on the head. Considering the weight of the cap stone, it would seem that more relief would be received in removing the stone from your head.

Ahenny is off the R697 Callan – Carrick on Suir road, about 6 km from Carrick and near to Kilkieran.

The route is well signposted and the crosses are in a walled churchyard across a field outside the village.

7 Kilkieran High Crosses

Kilkieran is a townsland and the graveyard is in the middle of a field beside the main road.

There are three sandstone crosses and the fragments of another high cross from the 9th century.

The West Cross, or decorated cross, (see right) is 3.8 meters high and is probably the most important. It is very similar to the crosses at Ahenny.

It is completely ornamented with interlacing along the shaft and arms with the exception of a panel on the west face with four long-necked beasts, with a small equal-armed cross in the centre.

On the north face of the base there are two chrysanthemum motifs. The east face of the base has two panels, each with four horsemen. The west face of the base has three panels, the centre one containing five swirls in a geometric arrangement.

The North Cross is unique with its tall, thin shape. It is 3.5 metres high with very short cross arms on a circular base. It may have had a cap on it, making it even taller. It has some mouldings on it.

The Plain cross is smaller at 2.8 metres. It has some mouldings and the central boss mimics studded metalwork in stone. It has a heavy mitre like crown.

In addition to the crosses there are several bullaun stones. These are stones with a depression which may be filled with water. They can have magical or religious significance.

One is built into the wall at St. Kieran's holy well nearby as a font for the cure of headaches.

The crosses are in a walled cemetery on the R698, which is just off the R697, the road from Callan to Carrick-on-Suir. The crosses are about 300m from the junction and well signposted.

Kilmogue Dolmen

Hidden up a short lane in the heart of the county, nestling between rolling hills of farm land and well away from modern motorways, stands Leac an Scail, which lays claim to be Ireland's tallest dolmen.

The Bronze Age dolmen can be hard to find as the signposts also call it the Harristown Dolmen although it is in the townland of Kilmogue. It is one of a number of dolmens in the south Kilkenny area. It is easily the largest and also the most accessible

A beast of a structure standing at 4.5m (15ft) high, the sheer physical size of the stones used makes one wonder at the person for whom it was built. Named Leac an Scail, (Stone of the Warrior or Hero), we can assume it was built for him and not by him, as it took the might of many people to put the dolmen together. As dolmens are burial chambers, we could assume that remains of the mighty hero are buried underneath it.

It is made up of a number of very large stones. A large granite capstone, resting on two equally large stones, sits on a pillow stone which rests on a back stone for extra stability. The capstone is almost 14m (45 ft) in circumference. The portal stones are 3.7m (12 ft) high and the capstone reaches 4.5m (15 ft). The entrance faces North East, away from the prevailing wind and it has an enormous door-stone 3m (10 ft) high.

When originally built it lacked the hedges and trees that make up the surrounding ditches and would have been visible from some distance.

The stones we see now would have originally been covered in earthen mounds, with the area below the capstone forming an entrance leading to the tomb proper. Hence the correct name of Portal Tombs.

Starting south on the R701 follow the sign for Hugginstown and Mullinavat. 10km south is a signpost pointing right to the Harristown Dolmen. About 2.5km is a cross roads with a sign post. 1km from here, take a left down a country lane and the Portal tomb is hidden behind some bushes at the bottom of the laneway.

9 Aghaviller & Castlemorris Estate

Aghaviller (Áth an Bhiolair, meaning "field of the watercress")

Outside Newmarket and on a spur of off the main road to Carrick-on-Suir lies the remains of the ancient monastic settlement of Aghaviller, dedicated to St. Brenainn. (Probably St. Brendan of Birr 6th c.)

In a graveyard, surrounded by a high wall lies the remains of a 12th century church with a 15th century residence attached. This large castle-like building is the most visible part of the site.

Aghaviller church with the shortened tower behind

Tall trees to the left make for a spooky visit especially if you visit near dusk.

At the rear, is the stump of one of the county's five round towers. This one is different from many round towers as it had two doors. Its circumference is just under 15.5 meters. The slate-coloured sandstone is beautifully coursed and dressed to the curve inside and out.

The almost level top is 9.6 meters above ground level at its highest point. If the original pillar-tower had the usual proportions of such building, it was in all probability about 33m high. The original NE-facing doorway is over 4 meters above the present ground level.

The ground level door is a recent addition. Standing inside the tower feels like stepping inside a wide chimney which can funnel the

sound of the crows and ravens from the nearby woods for added atmosphere.

An upper level of the residence attached to the church can be reached by a stairs within the wall. All that is left of the residence here is the remains of a stone fireplace. However, you can also view the shortened round tower from a height.

What remains of the original church is now below ground, with only foundations left.

Heading back towards the junction, and travelling 1km to the left you come to the grand gates of Castlemorris Estate, with parking opposite.

Once the estate of Viscount Mountmorris, this was one of the largest stately homes in the country and was built around 1751. It was said to have had 365 windows.

The family fortunes waned over the years and the only family members still in the area are buried in the family vault in Aghaviller churchyard, beside the round tower.

In 1924 the house was sold to the State but fell derelict. In the early 1930's it was unroofed and a demolition sale took place. The house was finally demolished in 1978. The grounds are now a part of Coillte woods totalling approximately 2,000 acres.

There are level walking trails from 3km to 7km around the main estate, although not suitable for buggies. The trails are well signposted.

The woods teem with wildlife and the trees are home to a variety of wild birds. In season, the estate is filled with wildflowers.

(For a map and details of this and other walking trails in Kilkenny go to Trailkilkenny.ie, download a walking app from the same site or look for the handy pack at a hotel or tourist office locally)

Aghaviller lies 1km south of Newmarket on a spur to the right, where the road veers off towards Carrick-on-Suir. The Castlemorris Estate surrounds the churchyard.

Kilree High Cross & Tower

The Kilree monastic site lies on the crest of a hill. It is surrounded by mature trees and dominated by a ruined round tower.

An ancient church ruin here is surrounded by gravestones covering centuries of the dead of the locality. Even the nave of the church was called into service at the start of the 20th century.

The High Cross is located in the field beyond the graveyard and tower. It is believed to be of the 9th century. It standing at 2.75 metres high. The sandstone cross is badly weathered. Most of it is covered with bosses, five on one side and one on the other, and geometrical motifs. Look closely at the East face and you may make out a hunting scene on the

arms. The ends of the South arm also has some shadowy figures. The figures on the west face may be Adoration of the Magi or Daniel in the Lions den. A tenon joint still visible suggests the cross originally had a capstone.

Predating the nearby priory in Kells, the round tower at 29m was built sometime between the 8th and 11th century and was mainly a bell tower for the nearby church.

The church of Kilree lies 3km from Kells village. The road is signposted at the entrance to the Priory car park. Entrance is free. The field has a sign warning of a bull. None has ever been seen.

Kells *(Ceannanus)*

The sleepy village of Kells 15km south of the city is home to Kells Priory. But more than this, the village also has two large mill building almost intact which can be viewed on the pretty riverside walk way from the priory to the village.

Close by, upriver, is the bridge which has five arches or eight arches depending on which side you are standing when you look at it. Built in 1725 and added to in 1775, it is worth a moment of your visit.

The village of Kells may be recognised by some older visitors who remember RTE's early drama series, The Riordans.

The fictional family and their neighbours lived in Leestown and, although much of the story was filmed in Co Meath, each series featured some outside filming in Kells where the writer Wesley Burrows lived near when he devised the show.

This was a revolutionary concept in the late 1960s where television programs were shooting was indoors, even the outdoor scenes.

The Riordans was later used by Yorkshire TV when developing their farm based series, Emmerdale. Some visitors may recognise the outside of 'Johnny Macs' and other buildings.

Kells Priory

Now a majestic ruin, the Priory is still the largest enclosed ecclesiastical site on the island, encompassing almost 3 acres (just over 1 ha). It has more history than Kilkenny Castle but is often overlooked by visitors to the county.

Access to the ruins is from a car park overlooking it from the Stoneyford Road. One of the most striking features is the seven tower houses at intervals along the surrounding curtain wall.

The first buildings put up by Geoffrey FitzRobert were ready in 1193 for four Augustinian monks from Bodmin in Cornwall to take over and administer as priests. They built their monastery in a hollow on an island that flooded and has since been filled with silt.

Over the next 150 years, the priory was attacked and burnt to the ground three times, including one visit by Edward Bruce of Scotland who picked Palm Sunday for his destruction.

The monks built stronger and higher walls and it became a monastic fortress. Kells flourished under the Cornishmens' leadership and the further West Country monks who followed them. It took over 100 years before a local, Elias of Shortallstown became prior.

Brother Walter Pembroke left a record in 1382 of his shopping list for April which included saffron, pepper, geese, pigs, wooden bowls, figs and oil for the lamps. Poverty obviously had its limits.

Times were still violent and in the 15th century the monks extended the priory walls to enclose more land so that locals could shelter their families and livestock when lawless bands harried the neighbourhood.

Inside the walls, good times continued for Brother Walter's successors for another century and a half but the Dissolution of the Priory under Henry VIII in 1540 saw the buildings and land transferred to the Earl of Ormond and its glory days were over. The last prior received a pension of £5 a year.

The large community that had grown up around the Priory lasted for some time afterwards but without the driving and guiding hands of the monks, the village lost its prominence.

The Priory is divided into two parts. The inner enclosure by the river, which contains most of the monastic remains, and a larger enclosure to the south home to tourists and sheep. Restoration work is being carried out gradually on the fabric of the building, but it can never regain the grandeur it must have displayed when at its peak in the Late Middle Ages.

One tower, the Prior's Tower has been brought back to life. A late construction in the life of the Priory and part of the south wall, it is four stories high and has a wooden roof which can be accessed complete with walkway and parapet, chimney and turret. Beware the stairs are steep.

After you have enjoyed the effigies, tomb stones and a walk around the perimeter, you can exit on the river side of the buildings and cross the bridge over the Kings River and stroll by the water side to see the two beautiful water mills, sadly not working at this time.

Mullins Mill on the Kings River at Kells.

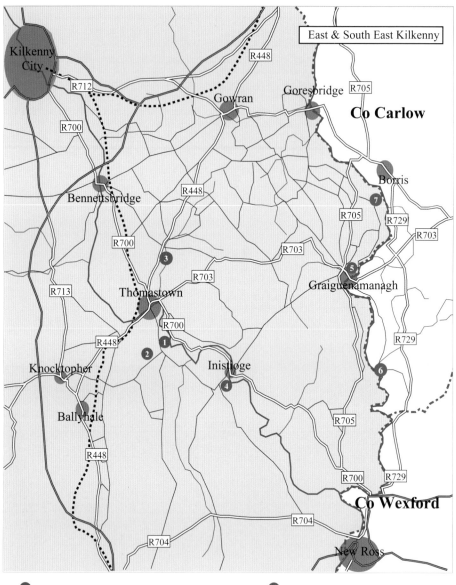

East & South East Kilkenny

1. Jerpoint Abbey
2. Newtown Jerpoint - Jerpoint Park
3. The Long Man of Kilfane
4. Woodstock House - Inistioge

5. Duiske Abbey - Graiguenamanagh
6. St. Mullins
7. Ullard Church

Thomastown (*Baile Mhic Andaín*)

Thomastown is located on a crossing point which was important since Norman times and only recently found relief from busy passing traffic with the opening of the M9 motorway.

In the early 13th Century, Thomas Fitzanthony, an Anglo-Norman mercenary, founded the town, replacing an existing Irish settlement.

He died in 1229, but almost 800 years later some remnants of his fortifications remain, in the towers still guarding the valuable bridge and Grennan Castle down river nearby.

Little else of FitzAnthony's town remains other than the shape of the central streets which form a square, best viewed from the car park near the church.

The other mark left is in the Gaelic name of the town which translates as Fitzanthony's town.

Grennan Castle from the Inistioge Road.

Outside of the town on the R700 road to Inistioge, there is a viewing point where you can stop and look at the ruins of the house that FitzAnthony built for himself. In good repair until the 1800s, the building is used today as little more than a shelter for grazing cattle.

With its proximity to the River Nore, Thomastown was a centre of milling for most of its life, as well as being a port for boats to carry goods to and from the port of New Ross.

This industry has died away and the last mill has been converted to house Grennan Craft School. This has become a focus for small craft based businesses which have located in the area.

Although a small town in its own right, it did produce one famous son, the philosopher Bishop George Berkeley (see page 109) and its cultural gift to the world was watercolourist,

Mildred Ann Butler. (see page 113).

In recent times, Thomastown has become a 'Town of Food', an initiative which aims to develop the food culture in the town.

It already boasts a Michelin Star restaurant in the Lady Helen at the Mount Juliet estate, adjacent to the town, as well as a number of local food producers.

> **Goatsbridge Trout Farm**
>
> Although a private commercial working farm, the Goatsbridge Trout farm located between Jerpoint Abbey and Newtown Jerpoint is worth a visit. You can get freshly caught rainbow trout from ponds fed by the Little Arrigle River or, for the more adventurous, try trout caviar.

Jerpoint Abbey

Jerpoint Abbey dominates its surroundings. Its warm biscuit coloured stone softens the massive presence of the building, which seems to bully its way on to the public road.

Built in 1158 by Donogh O'Donoghue Mac Gilla Padraig, the King of Osraige, for the Benedictine order, Jerpoint became home to the Cistercian order of monks twenty years later. Jerpoint still dominates its surrounding countryside with its large tower.

Although the place has fallen into ruins since the dissolution of the monasteries in the time of Henry VIII, it still retains some of the grandeur and peace that comes with rich monastery living.

Jerpoint was an important monastery and by 1228 there were 36 monks and 50 brothers in the abbey. A community this size added greatly to the wealth of an area.

The monastery had its own watermills and granaries in addition to the usual parts of a large monastery. By the time of the Dissolution it owned almost 1,800 acres of land (325 ha.).

The oldest parts of the abbey are the Irish-Romanesque transepts and chancel, which contains some faded wall paintings. The east window dates from the 14th century and the imposing crenulated central tower was added in the 15th century.

Wooden steps still follow the run of the night stairs used by the monks for their night prayers. By going up them, you will reach the roof and can look down on the Dublin-Waterford railway line nearby, a modern convenience which would not have helped the medieval monk get a good night sleep.

The true treasures of Jerpoint are the stone reliefs and carvings. The cloisters can still be walked and the stone carvings of knights in splendid armour, courtly ladies richly dressed, bishops in full regalia and fabulous beasts and dragons are plentiful and worth taking time over.

In the transept chapels there are some tombs which are decorated with carved tomb weepers, who mourned the loss of the person inside .The building was improved over time and shows a mix of architectural styles from late Norman to early English.

The abbey remains alive in an odd way with the adjacent grave yard remaining in modern use but only for those born in the locality.

The abbey is best appreciated with a guided tour which is available from the visitors centre adjacent to the site.

The Cloister and inner courtyard of Jerpoint today.

The Tomb Weepers: Many Christian saints are traditionally represented by a symbol associated with their life, these are known as attributes and help to identify them. The weepers in the image above are believed to be six of the apostles, each with their own attribute that may represent the way they were martyred. From the left , unknown apostle, St. Thomas with a lance, St. Simon with a saw, St. Bartholomew with folds of his own skin, he was flayed alive, St. Paul the apostle holding a sword, and another unidentified apostle.

Opening Hours : Early March - November: Daily 09.00 - 16:00. Seasonal opening hours outside of these months. Admission fee applies.

② Jerpoint Park (Newtown Jerpoint)

The centre piece of Jerpoint Park is Newtown Jerpoint, which is a medieval ghost town. It is on private land, near Jerpoint Abbey and little of the town remains to be seen today.

However, the folds and rises on the ground still show us where the two main streets met and where the houses were. Some ruins remain but time has not been kind.

Here was a vibrant town, with its twisty streets, lanes, and alleys, now all obliterated, blotted out and only remembered in dusty parchments and books.

It is located beside where the main crossing of the River Nore was 800 years ago and where the all-important toll booth was. It must have been a very happy place to live as the 27 houses in the hamlet were able to support 14 taverns.

Presumably the surplus pubs were to quench the thirst of the travellers who must have rested there and not the less observant of the monks from the nearby monastery. At one time, the town was a site of pilgrimage, as the local churchyard was said to contain the remains of St. Nicholas of Myra.

Local folklore for many centuries says that two knights returning from the Crusades brought home the saint's bones to Jerpoint. How they got them is best not asked.

The saint's supposed final resting place is still visible with a beautiful carved slab outside the ruined church today.

St. Nicholas of Myra was an early Christian born in Petra in modern Turkey. He had a reputation for kindness to children and also associated with ships and the sea.

He is usually shown with three bags, which symbolises the three bags of gold he dropped through the chimney of a poor man to provide dowries for his three daughters, who could marry rather than become slaves.

(The three bags are today replicated in the sign of three gold balls used by pawnbrokers, for whom he is also patron saint.)

Among his other virtues he was remembered as a gift giver. His feast day is in December, which was celebrated by, amongst other things, gift giving.

Put all this together and you can see that St. Nicholas of Myra is the St. Nicholas every child still waits for each Christmas.

Nearby Belmore House is the starting point and in the summer time, the tea rooms provide a place to taste some home baking, after trying angling or other activities laid on by the hosts.

To get here, pass Jerpoint Abbey, travelling south and turn right towards Mount Juliet. The entrance is 500m along this road, on the right. Admission fee applies, and a guided tour for groups can be arranged.

③ The Long Man of Kilfane

Kilfane church and its surrounding woods are home to a rookery, which adds a gothic atmosphere to your visit.

The church still has some of its decorative features with ogee stones (curved like an S) over the three original doorways. There are also an altar, a piscine, a book rest and a 13th century sedilia, or stone seat, near the altar, which may have come from an earlier church at the site.

The church has a three-storied fortified presbytery attached which can be entered. Take care however in climbing to the upper floors as the noise of the crow families inhabiting the gaps and spaces in the building can make you feel very unwelcome.

Kilfane's most unique feature is an effigy of a Norman knight carved from a single slab of limestone. It is believed to represent Thomas de Cantwell (d. 1319), a Norman adventurer who became Lord of Kilfane.

The effigy is thought to have been a sarcophagus slab which has since been set upright against an inner wall of the church.

If the effigy is life size, then Thomas has earned his name of the Cantwell Fada or the Long Man. At near 2.4m tall (almost 8 ft) he would have been a giant.

He is shown wearing a suit of chain mail, with his legs crossed, right over left. This is believed to be a sign that he took part in a Holy Crusade, although it also looks like he has been caught short. He carries a shield on his left hand, bearing the arms of the Cantwell family. The Long Man is the tallest of his kind on the British Isles.

4km north of Thomastown, along the R448 road to Dublin is a turn to the right, signposted for Kilfane Church. 0.5km up this quiet country road, you come to a 19th century church and across the road is a small gate leading to a short woodland walk to the church of Kilfane.

Kilfane Glen and Waterfall

A further 2km past Kilfane Church is the entrance to Kilfane Glen & Waterfall. Here you will find a 6ha (15 acre) listed Irish Heritage Garden.

Forgotten and overgrown for many years, it is being restored to its full 18th century glory.

In addition to a fine 200 year old romantic garden is a dramatic 10m (30 ft) waterfall, gushing streams, tiny bridges and a small thatched rustic cottage. The grounds are crossed by gravel paths bounded by mosses and ferns, leading you through a number of themed gardens.

The gardens are private but opened to the public in July and August from 11am to 6pm. Admission fee applies. Phone 056-7724558 for more information or try www.kilfane.com

Inistioge *(Inis Tíog)*

Beside the slow moving River Nore, Inistioge is located on the limit of the tidal reach of the Atlantic. As a result, in medieval times, it was an important staging post bringing goods from the coast to Kilkenny and other inland towns.

Over 1,000 years ago a battle between the Danes and the Irish was fought here with 707 reported to have died. Surely a mighty battle at that time.

Possibly founded by the Vikings, who would have exploited the tidal each of the river to this point, the settlement was recognised by the Normans for its strategic location and developed.

A mark of its importance was an early establishment of an Augustinian community there.

Today's town owes much more to the building of the Woodstock estate which floats above the town. This was started in the 18th century and flowered in the 19th century.

The town benefited from the patronage of the Tighe family, the grandest of the owners. The tidy village green, with its two small monuments, harks back to a gentrified Anglo Irish time.

The town attracts many families in the summer who gather by the small park near the bridge to watch the slow passage of the river.

The bridge was built in 1763 after a great flood destroyed the original and many others on the river.

An architectural feature is the contrast between both sides. The upriver or town side has triangular cutwaters to deal with any future

The River Nore at Inistioge

floods but the gentler down river side is decorated with Ionic pilasters, showing some of the Classical style of the time.

The tidal reach is just short of the bridge and in 1999 this was dramatically highlighted when a salt water dolphin found its way to the town. After a large rescue operation, it was returned to the sea.

The land by the river forms part of a local flood plain and the river is rich in lampreys and crayfish as well as salmon.

Angling is one of the big attractions for locals and visitors and summer evenings can find the banks thronged with relaxed anglers.

For those who have the time to enjoy the activity, there is a 3km walk along the river side below the woods of the Woodstock estate. It starts beside O'Donnells' pub in the Square and the estate can be accessed from the walk.

There is a map on the village green which shows the varied walking routes.

 # Woodstock House

For generations the home of the Tighe family, the mansion that was Woodstock House, is now a ruin. It was originally built in the 1700's by Sir William Fownes, who had inherited the estate.

He used it to gain social position with the local gentry and it must have worked as he married Lady Elizabeth Ponsonby, the daughter of the Earl of Bessborough. Their only child Sarah married William Tighe and the estate remained in the Tighe family name from that time.

The Tighe family appear to have been good landlords providing schools for Catholic and Protestant children, endowing both their churches and managing the estates without evictions.

By the mid 19th century Woodstock had modest formal gardens designed by the original architect. Then came Lady Louisa. She expanded and improved the existing gardens, the terraced rockeries and created the remarkable arboretum.

This contains specimen trees from across Asia and South America and she created two formal walks using Monkey Puzzle trees and Noble Firs.

She is said to have given away two thirds of her income each year to help the poor and needy of the locality. She started a lace making business for local employment.

She was a truly remarkable woman. At the age of 12 she buckled the sword around the waist of her godfather, the Duke of Wellington, at a ball her mother held in Brussels on the eve of the Battle of Waterloo. She died in 1900, just short of her 100th birthday.

Sadly, the heyday of Woodstock was nearing and end. In 1921, during the War of Independence, it was used as a base for the Black & Tans and Auxiliaries, two quasi military parts of the Royal Irish Constabulary at the time and much resented for the atrocities they inflicted on ordinary citizens across the country.

In the Civil War that followed, the house was gain used as a base, this time by the Free State Army. They were withdrawn from the area on July 1st 1922 and the following day, the unguarded house was set alight and burnt to the ground.

The house today remains a ruin but the true treasure of Woodstock, which was Lady Louisa's gardens, have been restored and open to the public.

Woodstock Garden is a mix of formal and informal. It includes a walled garden, a terraced garden, a rose garden and a Yew walk.

The Nobel Fir Walk

It has two stunning wooded avenues; one of Monkey Puzzle and one of Nobel Fir trees.

An arboretum was the focus of exotic tree planting in the 19th century. It has Asian and South American specimen trees and is dominated by conifers. Work is regularly carried out to ensure the survival of these important trees.

Open: 9.00 - 19.00 (summer months. 10.00 - 16.00 (winter months). Admission: Small charge per car for all occupants. Guided tours can be arranged by contacting the Head Gardener @ 087-8549785. www.woodstock.ie. Tea rooms are open during the summer.

Entrance to the Walled Garden

Graiguenamanagh *(Gráigh na Manach)*

In Irish, the name is 'village of the monks' and Graiguenamanagh certainly had a lot of monks in its time.

Known locally as Graigue, the town is located on the border with Co Carlow, the county boundary being formed by the River Barrow which separates Graigue from the village of Tinnahinch on the Carlow side of the river.

In the 17th century, Graigue straddled a significant highway as the River Barrow was a busy route for barges carrying goods to and from the ports of New Ross and Waterford. This trade continued into the mid 20th century but no longer continues.

The stone quays and lock gates near the bridge are relics of this time and now used as a stopping point for pleasure boats. The towpaths, left from that time, allow for long rewarding walks along by the river.

It is at the foot of Brandon Hill, which lays claim as the highest point in county Kilkenny (515m) and a favourite destination for hill walkers, being part of the South Leinster Way with unbroken trails north and south of the town for 25 miles.

Modern Graigue values the river and it is popular for boating, canoeing, swimming and fishing through the summer. The town also has a regatta on the river on the August Bank holiday weekend each year.

For one weekend each September, the town is host to an annual Town of Books festival during which music, walks, talks and family events bring this quiet little town to life.

 ## Duiske Abbey

The jewel of Graiguenamanagh is Duiske Abbey, a 13th century building, once the largest Cistercian abbey in the country. The name Duiske comes from the anglicisation of its Irish name 'Dubh Uisce' or Black Water.

The Abbey was originally founded in 1204 by William Marshall, the Earl of Pembroke, when he brought monks from the South of England, as part of the early Norman colonisation of Ireland.

In just over 20 years, the abbey had grown to housing 36 monks and a small army of lay brothers. The community had become so large that the Abbot sat in parliament at the time.

It prospered with the town for centuries until Henry VIII suppressed the monastery as part of the Reformation of the English church. The abbot resigned, as many did, but some of the monks continued to live in the buildings. Inevitably, over time the community fell apart and the buildings fell into ruins.

The church remained in use as a place of worship by the Church of Ireland but even so, deterioration continued and the tower fell into the church in 1744.

Eventually the church was handed to the Catholic community as a place of worship in

The simple interior of Duiske Abbey

93

1812. It wasn't until over a century later that restoration started and was completed in 1980. The present church is only a shadow of the glory and size of the original abbey. It was built with imported limestone.

At the entrance is the stone figure of a Norman knight carved in great details inevitably holding a sword. Some of the early medieval floor tiles are still visible. The building features Gothic and Romanesque architectural features.

Some of the original 13th century stonework has survived with leaf foliage carved into the capital, banded shafts setting off the plain white interior and dog-toothed ornaments.

There is a model of how the monastery looked at its peak on display inside which gives some idea of the size of the community.

Two Irish High Crosses are located outside; the Ballyogan cross and the Akythawn cross.

Some monks have returned to Graiguenamanagh showing their skills in writing, sheep shearing, harvesting grain and dairying.
These are part of a series of 12 monks spread around the town.

The River Barrow

The South Leinster Way is one of the major walking routes in the country. It is 104km long and stretches from Kildavin in Co Kildare to Carrick-on-Suir in Co Tipperary.

For part of the way, from Borris on the Kilkenny / Carlow border to Graiguenamanagh, it travels beside the River Barrow.

While the main walk then branches off across the hills to Inistioge, the riverside walk continues on the Carlow side to the small town of St. Mullins, which is a very popular 6.2 km walk.

The 12km walk from Borris passes through woodlands and beside old mills, much of it along an old tow path.

This stretch of the Barrow is a good place for bird watching. You'll almost certainly see kingfishers, several species of duck and many smaller birds also.

There are a few swimming spots also along the river, the safest being in Graiguenamanagh where there is a life guard on duty during the summer.

The River is also popular with people who like to cruise its shady waters in barges or boats through the summer. Graiguenamanagh is a popular stop off point for these river people.

The bridge over the River Barrow at Graiguenamanagh, with Brandon Hill in the distance.

6 St. Mullins *(Tigh Moling)*

Near Graiguenamangh, on the Carlow side f the river is the village of St. Mullins, named after St. Moling, who founded a monastery there in the 7th century.

He is reputed to have been a Gaelic prince who was also a poet, artist and craftsman. All these skills would have helped him as it is said he built the monastery with the help of the legendary ' Gobán Saor'.

Legend has it that the saint built a mile long watercourse to power his mill with his own hands, a task which took him 7 years. His hard work on the watercourse paid off as it still survives.

The saint died in 697 and is said to be buried in the Tempall Mor, the Great Church.

An 8th century manuscript, the Book of Moling, shows a plan of the original monastery. However, it was plundered by Vikings in 951 and burned in 1138. As a result the buildings no longer exist and were replaced in time. The site remained a popular place of worship and community and there are traces of three out of six original churches on the site. The most recent is a small Church of Ireland building from 1811, which now houses a local museum. In the height of the plague known as the Black Death, which ravaged Europe from 1348-50 , St. Mullins was a popular destination for those who thought that pilgrimage and prayer would protect them.

Sadly, by gathering in

The remains of the monastery site at St. Mullins, now a large graveyard filled with the remains of centuries of the local population.

large numbers to travel to the monastery, they only managed to create an even greater chance of catching the disease from infected fleas carried by other pilgrims.

By returning infected from the pilgrimage, they only helped to carry the plague to their own communities.

St. Moling is still remembered today. On the Sunday before the 17th June each year, there is a patron day where people visit and pray at St. Moling's Well, in the hope of finding cures for sickness and disease.

A 9th century Celtic High cross stands outside this newer building which is a reminder of the place's past glory.

The surrounding graveyard contains some graves of those who fought in the 1798 rebellion.

There are remains of other medieval buildings still there together with a dramatic Norman motte.

A motte was a huge earthen mound, on top of which the Normans built a wooden fortification. Beside this was built a bailey, a fortified area on the ground, in which the soldiers and out buildings were located.

Mottes dominated the surrounding area providing a place to attack from and a stronghold to defend. Traces of the bailey can still be seen.

7 Ullard

At Ullard are the roofless remains of a small 12th century medieval church. While never as grand as nearby Duiske Abbey, built a little later, Ullard has been a Christian settlement for much longer. Records suggest that St. Fiacre founded a monastery here in the 6th century. Worn heads over the Romanesque doorway are said to be him and St. Moling, who built the church. The Church is built on sloping ground and a vault beneath the east end might have been designed to compensate for this by raising the floor to the same level as the west end or Nave.

The church has been 'improved' over time with some 16th century additions. The most awkward is the extension at the rear which involved the addition of a 20th century handball court. At its corner stands a granite High Cross with weather worn but barely recognizable carving.

On the Cross head itself is the Crucifixion, flanked by David with his Harp on the left, the Sacrifice of Isaac on the right and two unknown figures above (it is said the unknown figures are of Sts. Paul and Anthony). On the cross shaft itself are carvings of Adam and Eve and of six Apostles.

The graveyard around contains 18th century headstones featuring simple carving. Ullard can be translated as 'Apple Garden'.

Doorway to Ullard Church

From Graiguenamanagh take R705 north for about 5km, then take a right turn, sign-posted for Ullard Church. It is approximately 1km down this narrow road on the left. There is a small car park here with room for a few cars. Open daily, admission free.

North Co Kilkenny

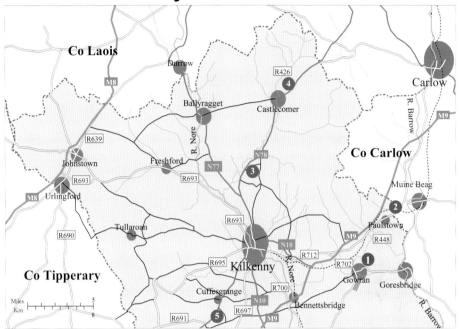

1 St. Mary's Church, Gowran

2 Shankill Castle, Paulstown

3 Dunmore Cave

4 Castlecomer Demesne

5 Burnchurch Tower House

Gowran *(Gabhrán)*

Gowran is a village 15Km east of Kilkenny city. In its golden days, which were before the Normans arrived, it was a royal residence of the Kings of Ossory.

Once they were ousted and the Normans took over, it looked as if things would get even better. They created a Barony covering modern East Kilkenny, with Gowran at its head. As was customary, they built a fine church on the site of a former monastery.

However, things took a turn for the worse in 1316 when the army of Edward Bruce took the town in brutal fashion as part of their long march from Ulster . It was part of a futile attempt to take over the country.

In 1385, things looked up again when

James, the 3rd Earl of Ormond, moved into a castle he had built there but six years later he bought Kilkenny Castle and moved permanently out of the area.

Gowran's prospects floundered for a time. In 1578, a magdalene hospital was built there for the "relief of poor leprous people", who must have been in abundance.

In 1608, King James I made it a parliamentary borough, with its own member of parliament, setting Gowran on the path to fortune once more.

Just when it looked as if Gowran was about to move up in the world, another disaster struck when it found itself in the path of a righteous, unforgiving Cromwellian army in 1650.

97

Cromwell laid siege and eventually the soldiers of the garrison accepted his offer of quarter for their lives and handed over their officers.

Cromwell ordered the execution by firing squad of all but one of the officers; a priest captured in the castle, who was hanged.

In 1688, fortune's wheel turned once more when James II granted a Charter incorporating Gowran as a town with 18 burgesses. This was a step up for Gowran. However, this was as good as it got. The town never really grew from then.

1914 saw the first race meeting at Gowran Park race course, just outside the village. It hosts National Hunt and Flat meetings and its signature race, the Thyestes Chase, held each January, is seen as an early warm up for the Aintree Grand National each year.

St. Mary's Church

In the centre of Gowran stands the sturdy remains of a church built in 1260, when the Normans were at the peak of church building. Unusually, this one was not run by monks or friars but by a college of priests who lived beside it.

Now incorporated into St. Mary' Protestant church, the large and more elaborate original consists of a nave (where the people sat) with an aisle and a long chancel (where the altar was placed).

Remains of the high quality sculpture in the building can be seen throughout including carved masks.

Much of this early work was created by an unnamed master mason known now as the Gowran Master. His work has also been identified in St. Canice's Cathedral in Kilkenny, which was built around the same time. As a sculptor, he was probably the most gifted craftsman in Ireland in the 13th century.

In the 19th century the church tower was incorporated into the new parish church, which was built in place of the chancel and which now takes up about half of the building. This was only one of many changes made over the centuries.

The tower and 19th century church are now a visitor's centre and they house a number of carved effigies and tombstones from early times.

There are 14th century effigies of a man and wife, probably representing James Butler, the first Earl of Ormond, buried here in 1382 and Lady Eleanor de Bohun. Also there is the 13th century effigy of a priest and a 16th century altar tomb of the Butlers. From much further back in time, there is a cross-inscribed ogham stone.

Lastly, there is an effigy of Sadhbh MacMurrough-Kavanagh, daughter of the King of Leinster and wife of Sir James Butler of Paulstown.

In the 1920's, a remembrance window to Aubrey Cecil White was donated by his mother. Aubrey was one of the thousands of Irish who lost their lives in the Great War of 1914-18 and his body was never recovered from where it fell in the Battle of the Somme in 1916. The poignant figure of the young soldier beneath the badge of his regiment was made by artist Michael Healy, a member of An Túr Gloine.

Shankill Castle, Paulstown *(Baile Phóil)*

Shankill Castle is in Paulstown, 16km from Kilkenny City on the R712 to Carlow. It started as a tower-house built by a lesser ranch of the Butler family (in the sixteenth century), near the ruins of an old church.

In 1708 it was rebuilt in a less austere style and was set in a formal landscape. The striking vista at the front and the ornamental canal to the rear were softening additions.

In the 19th century, it was enlarged and castellated. Serpentine bays were added to the canal and an unusual polyhedral sundial given pride of place on a sunken lawn.

The interior preserves much of its 18th century character and features including a Georgian staircase, Gothic plaster work and a Victorian drawing room. Shankill is nothing if not universal in style.

For those who love gardens, Shankill has the same eclectic mix outdoors. From a moated garden to trees sown in the 18th, 19th and 20th century, depending on the fashions of the time there is plenty of interest.

Since 1991 Shankill Castle is home and studio to the artist Elizabeth Cope, whose paintings are on display. Shankill is also an artist's retreat where those whose muse needs nurturing can stay and seek inspiration, with workspace and accommodation available.

The grounds and gardens are open to the public and there are guided tours of the house. As it is also a family home, opening times can change at short notice.

Shankill Castle is home to a few ghosts. However, the most ghostly story relates to a curse put on the estate by a hunted priest left to die on the lane outside. Before he passed away, he said "Grass will grow on this avenue and these gates will never close".

The view of the Castle from the road, outside of Paulstown, shows the grass covered avenue leading to gates. These gates were closed each night after the priests death, but found open the next morning. Even when chained closed, they were open at day break. Eventually the gates were set in concrete, as can be seen today *.... and they are still not closed properly.*

Opening Times:
Apr. - May Sat &
Sun 11am to 5pm.
Jun. - Aug Thurs to
Sun. 11am to 5pm.
Sept.- Oct. Sat &
Sun 11am to 5pm..
Closed Nov - Mar,
Grounds only
Apr.- Oct 11am to
5pm
Entrance fees
apply.

Gate Lodge to Shankill Castle in Paulstown

Dunmore Cave *(Dearc Fhearna)*

Eleven kilometres north of Kilkenny City, on the Castlecomer road you will find Dunmore Caves, formed of limestone over 300 million years.

Although this is smaller than many of the caves around the country, the series of chambers formed over millions of years, the magic of the rock formations, as well as its historical interest make it one of Ireland's more fascinating caves.

In approx 3,500 BC, the effects of erosion, caused the limestone rock to collapse and the caves we see today came into being. It contains almost a quarter of a mile of passages and at its deepest point is 150 foot below the surface.

Over the centuries, various human bones have been found here and an ancient 9th century Irish text, 'The Annals of the Four Masters', mentions a Viking massacre here. This was disputed over time but study of the bones, which come from nineteen female adults and twenty-five children and the find of jewellery and personal possessions found hidden in cracks in the stone in recent years, have confirmed the story of what happened.

A raiding Viking band attacked a small village near Dunmore, and the frightened inhabitants fled to hide in the nearby cave for safety. However, it proved to be a trap. The Vikings found them and lit fires at the cave entrance, using the smoke to drive them out.

The men were taken as slaves, but the women and children were killed or left in the cave to die. The jewellery and other items were a last pathetic attempt by the victims to save the last of what they had by hiding them. Sadly, they remained hidden for 1,000 years.

Since 1940, it has been a National Monument and stairs, walkways and an extensive lighting system have been installed. There is little plant and animal life in and around the cave mainly due to the lack of sunlight. There are exhibitions and displays in the Visitor Centre.

The entrance to the cave is by way of steps so it is not suitable for wheelchairs or buggies and, with lots of steps to negotiate, a reasonably sturdy pair of legs are needed. However, there is no dangerous climbing to do.

Opening Times: Wednesday to Sunday inclusive 9:30 - 17:30,
Closed Monday and Tuesday but open on Bank Holidays.
Last admission 15:00.   Admission: fees apply.

Castlecomer *(Caisleán an Chumair)*

The name translates as the Castle at the Confluence of the Waters. Castlecomer is built where the rivers Deen, Brocagh and Cloghogue meet.

The first Normans settlers built a castle there in 1171, on the lands owned by the Brennan clan. Since then its history has been marked with conflict.

By 1200, the Brennans decided to remove the newcomers and burnt the castle and surrounding settlement. The settlement which replaced it was in turn burnt by William de Bermingham in 1328.

On the fault line between Gaelic and Anglo-Norman Ireland, the town continued to be a place of dispute and discord over the following centuries.

By the 1600s, the exploitation of the local coal mines by the Wandesforde family had begun. As they grew wealthy on the mines' profits, a planned town was built.

In 1641, the Confederation forces besieged it, bringing more fire and destruction. In 1798, the town was again attacked, this time by rebel forces from Wexford marching towards Dublin. Again Castlecomer was partly burned to the ground.

Meanwhile, King Coal brought prosperity to he region. The family seat of the Wandesfordes remained here and the family invested heavily in the locality.

During the Famine, the family paid for 3,000 people to emigrate to the Americas. Debate continues as to whether this was a deed of charity or an opportunistic clearance of the lands.

Castlecomer became the main market town of north Kilkenny and an 'estate village' for the family. Its signature feature is the magnificent, broad lime-tree lined Square with Georgian houses.

Prosperity continued until the mid 20th century, when the extraction of the coal began to lose its profit and, in 1969, the mines closed up.

Each New Year's Day, Castlecomer hosts a Wellie Race. Contestants run a 5km route through the countryside wearing wellington boots. Fiercely contested, the race raises money for local and national charities and its mention in the Guinness Book of records was the impetus for many similar events around the world.

Anthracite coal has been commercially mined in the Castlecomer region since about 1640 and it continued for over 300 years. The main promoters of the mine were the Wandesforde family and their enterprise made them very wealthy. Originally, iron ore was mined but just as the last of the iron was being extracted, a seam of coal was struck. Coal had been found in small amounts before this, but the Wandesfordes had the ability and money to exploit it.

Much of the first mining was of a 1m (3ft) seam near the surface, with two further seams, The Jarrow and the Skehana seams mined later as the enterprise expanded. By the start of the 19th century, there were 16 mines operating in the area.

No explosives existed when mining first started, so that to get at the coal, the overlying rock had to be broken by wedges, hammers and so on. Coal was extracted by hand and brought through the underground tunnels on timber sleighs.

A hundred year's later, when the first seam was near exhausted, the Jarrow seam was discovered and developed using explosives and work was made easier by the introduction of steam power.

The lowest seam, Skehana, was opened and mined in the 20th century. From the 1940's mining was being carried out mainly by machinery. By the time the mines closed in 1969, 11 miles of underground roadways had been built. At its peak, between the two world wars, local employment due to the mines reached 1,000. All this was lost when they eventually closed causing wide-scale economic damage to Castlecomer and its surrounding villages.

For more visit the 'Footprints in Coal' exhibition at the Discovery Park.

Castlecomer Demesne & Discovery Park

Part of the legacy of the Wandesfordes is the 2.5 ha (80a) demesne, which was once the estate farmyard, gardens, stable yard and leisure grounds. It is now home to Castlecomer Discovery Park. Castlecomer House, the family home, was located on the opposite side of the N78 road.

The original house was built in 1638 and was burned down during the Battle of Castlecomer in 1798.

A bigger house was built in its place in 1802 during the time of Lady Anne Ormonde. Most of the building was demolished in 1975 as it was no longer in use and had fallen into disrepair. Nothing now remains of the house.

The Visitor Centre is located in what was originally the farm yard and kitchen gardens of the estate. The stables and many of the farm buildings have been restored and now house a craft yard of workshops and studios. There is also a mining and science museum.

Outside, the original walled garden is now home to a small herd of Fallow and Sika Deer and a flock of Jacob Sheep.

Beside this, embedded in the Demesne, is a bid adventure park to pump up your adrenaline. Popular activities include the tree top adventure walk, with a path through the trees 10m off the ground. In addition, there is a climbing wall and a chance to take the Leap of Faith from the top of a 7m pole.

For those less faint of heart, the park also has a 300m zip wire that crosses the woods and two lakes at a height of 35m in parts. Finally, there is the octagon high rope course. For your inner Viking, there is archery and axe throwing.

You might also come across groups trying their hand at raft or catapult building.

There is also a woodland adventure trail with climbing and rope swinging for younger visitors and, deep in the woods lies a fairy and elf village to be explored.

For most people, the big attractions are the walking trails, which circle two lakes. There are four looped walks from 1.5km to 5km and all but the longest are suitable for buggies.

The walks include a sculpture trail and the remains of a ruined castle at the farthest part of the park.

Originally constructed by the Prior Wandesforde family, the two man-made lakes formed a centrepiece for their demesne. A series of cascades link the lakes and channel the water back into the River Deen.

Having been drained in the past, the lakes are now fully re-instated and are stocked with trout. In addition, you can go boating and canoeing on the lake..

The demesne is located just north of the town on the Dublin Road. Entry is free with a nominal €2 charged for all day parking.

Discovering a Fairy House

Overleaf: Tackling the Octagon High Ropes.

Burnchurch Tower House

Burnchurch Castle is a 15th Century tower house built by the Fitzgerald family and was occupied until the 1817. Looking cold and forbidding, tower houses were the must have properties when first built.

Unlike the castles, designed to house the Lord, his household retainers, and soldiers, tower houses were essentially family homes of the better-off land owners.

They were built by Irish and Anglo-Norman alike. They were usually tall rectangular towers, with four or five storeys. Burnchurch has six.

Inside, there was usually only one main room on each floor. At least one of the floors consisted of a stone vault, while the others were of timber.

In many examples the vault formed the floor of the main upper room of the tower house, which was the main reception room of the building at the top of the stairs. In many cases this had a central fireplace and was open to the roof, where a louvre took away the smoke.

The family lived on the upper two floors and the servants occupied the vaulted basement or it was used for storage. Furniture and comfort was not to our standard but, while frugal, was probably better than the peasant neighbours.

The roof was usually surrounded by a parapet with stepped crenellations behind which the occupants could defend the building against attackers. Burnchurch has the characteristic Irish-style of stepped battlements.

A spiral stairs or lengths of straight stairs within the walls gave access to the upper floors. Burnchurch has an unusually large number of passages and chambers hidden inside the walls.

The ground floor entrance was usually well defended. This could be by section of the parapet projecting directly above the door through which rocks could be dropped on attackers, as it is here, or a murdering hole inside the door, which could be used in the same way if attackers had penetrated that far, or an outer grill of iron secured on the inside with a chain, which protected the main wooden door.

A great hall was formerly attached to the tower's outside wall, but this has now vanished. All that survives is a 12.5m tall turret from one corner.

The towers were sometimes contained within a bawn or defensive wall, which helped keep cattle from wandering even if it failed to repel attackers. That of Burnchurch has disappeared.

Tower house building reached its peak in the fifteenth and sixteenth centuries. Perhaps the most famous Irish example is Bunratty Castle in Co. Clare

To get there. Travel from Kilkenny on the N76 towards Callan. 7km out is a turn to the left. It is notable for having a tree grow in the middle of the junction.

Burnchurch is 2km along this road, The tower can not be entered and only viewed from outside.

Bluebell sculpture by the roadside.

Kilkenny
People

To name but a few.

As with any place one visits, what gives a place its true character is its people. In your travels, you will meet the current crop of Kilkenny residents. You will find them to be generally a quiet modest people, whose blood rarely rises unless there is a hurley nearby.

While people in the city can suffer at times from the modern disease of time pressure, the country side allows for a more relaxed approach to life and you should find many who will have the time to stop and talk.

Some individuals however, stand out above the throng. Like any community, there are those whose lives made a difference well beyond their own town or village. For some, it needed a generation or two for the name to flower. Kilkenny has those and in the following pages you will meet a few.

Not all will be known to you but you should meet someone whose name or whose life's work you will have come across. A short history of Kilkenny's most influential family, the Butlers, includes black sheep and saints.

To show that we are broadminded in Kilkenny, we have even included one or two blow-ins and one who isn't human but whose name may be the best known of all.

Bishop George Berkeley

Churchman and philosopher (1685 - 1753)

George Berkeley was born at Dysart, Thomastown and educated at Kilkenny College and later Trinity College Dublin. He remained there after he completed his degree and began to publish books on mathematics and early works on optics.

In 1710, he published a 'Treatise Concerning the Principles of Human Knowledge' in which he posed the idea that nothing exists outside the mind. His next work, the snappily titled "Three Dialogues between Hylas and Philonous", developed the idea.

He now suggested that the world we know through our senses only exists because we perceive it. In other words, everyday objects around us are not material items but ideas in our minds. Simply put, things only exists if we can see, hear, smell or touch them.

His ideas formed part of the launch pad for many of the works of later philosophers, as well as researchers in the areas of physics, mathematics, optics and moral philosophy.

His work was widely read in his lifetime but his work gathered influence in the years after his death. German philosopher Arthur Schopenhaur called him the father of idealism.

His ideas and system are regarded as clearing the way for later thinkers such as Kant and David Hume and study of his ideas continues to grow even into the 21st century.

In 1721, he took holy orders and began to advance through the church ranks. In 1728, he married and moved to live in Rhode Island in America soon after.

While there he drew up plans for a city he wanted to build in Bermuda. The city never happened and he returned to London four years later.

America remembered this son of Kilkenny. A town was named after him in Massachusetts and, a century later, a city was also named for him in California, where there is now a famous university.

In 1734, he was appointed Bishop of Cloyne, in Cork, where he lived, merrily thinking and publishing until his death in 1753.

Berkeley's immaterialism was summed up in a pair of gently mocking limericks by Msgr. Ronald Knox:

There was a young man who said, "God
Must think it exceedingly odd
If he finds that this tree
Continues to be
When there's no one about in the Quad."

REPLY
Dear Sir:
Your astonishment's odd:
I am always about in the Quad.
And that's why the tree
Will continue to be,
Since observed by, Yours faithfully,
GOD.

(Quad: An open quadrangle or courtyard, associated with schools and universities.)

ÉIRE 44

Bishop George Berkeley 1685-1753

Reproduced by kind permission of An Post ©

The Butlers of Ormonde

In 1185, Prince John, brother of Richard 1 came to Ireland. In his entourage was Theobald Walter, an English nobleman. John gave him a large area of Irish land and the important job of Chief Butler of Ireland. In old French, a botellier was an officer in charge of the king's wine bottles, derived from boteille meaning bottle.

Theobald's job was to make sure there was plenty of food and drink ready for the king and his followers when he visited Ireland.

The Butlers were also given the 'Prisage' of Wine. This entitled them to 10% of all the wine that was imported to Ireland and was the basis of the family wealth for centuries.

A final honour for the Chief Butler was that he had to serve the first glass of wine to the king after he had been crowned. This is what the three cups on the Butler crest stands for.

Theobald's surname changed to Walter le Boteler, which eventually became Butler.

Much of their land was in County Tipperary. At that time the area was known as Oir Mhumhan in Irish, which meant east Munster. This is how we get the word 'Ormond', used in the noble titles of the Butlers.

James. 1st Earl of Ormond.
Tomb stone at St Mary's Church
Gowran

In 1327, the 7th Chief Butler, James, married Eleanor, a niece of Edward III. Soon after, the King made him 1st Earl of Ormond. He died in 1338 and the engraved stone in St Mary's Church, Gowran, may be of him. At this time the Butlers were living in Gowran Castle.

James's grandson James became the 3rd Earl and bought Kilkenny Castle and its lands in 1391.

The family became very rich. Thomas, the 7th Earl was known as the Wool Earl due to the main source of his wealth. Besides owning most of Kilkenny and Tipperary, he owned 72 manors in England, making him one of the richest subjects in the realm.

One of his daughters, Margaret, married Sir Thomas Boleyn in England. Their granddaughter, Ann Boleyn, was the second wife of King Henry VIII and their great-granddaughter was Queen Elizabeth I of England.

His son James was murdered in 1497 by his cousin Piers Rua, or Red Piers, who became the 8th Earl. Piers' wife came from another powerful Irish family, the Fitzgeralds of Kildare.

From their tomb in St Canice's Cathedral (overleaf), we see how the rich in Ireland dressed in the mid 16th century.

Their son, James, the 9th Earl, bought vast amounts of land which had come on the market after Henry VIII closed the monasteries in Ireland in 1537. He didn't get to enjoy them long, as he and his servants were victims of a mass poisoning at a feast in London, in 1546.

His son, 'Black' Tom, became the 10th Earl. Queen Elizabeth I was very friendly with her Butler cousin, calling him her black husband and made him Treasurer of Ireland. Black Tom's son and heir died while he was only six.

110

His other child was Elizabeth. Kilkenny Castle and all its estates could only be owned by a man, so to make sure that his daughter would inherit his castle and property, Tom arranged for her to marry a Butler cousin called Theobald. Ten years later Theobald died before Tom, leaving her a widow.

As they had no children, the title would go to Black Tom's cousin, Walter. He lived in Kilcash Castle in Co. Tipperary on the slopes of Slievenamon. A fervent Catholic, he was known as Walter of the Beads.

He was one of the leaders of the Old English in the Irish Parliament. Kilkenny Castle and all its land would also go to him.

Elizabeth had been looking forward to living in the Castle and being the lady of a great estate. This was not possible any more unless she could get the King to allow her inherit the property.

She married Robert Preston, a Scottish nobleman, hoping his Court connections would help her gain back her lands.

Black Tom died and Walter became the 11th Earl. Elizabeth started the court case.

Thanks to the contacts she had made in court, she was able to persuade King James I to allow her to inherit. Walter was left with the manor in Gowran, along with a small amount of land.

Walter knew that the only way that he could become owner of Kilkenny Castle and lands again, was to persuade the king to change his mind. He asked James I to admit that he had made a mistake. Enraged that his decision was questioned, the King threw Walter in prison, where he spent the next eight years.

When Walter was finally released, Charles I was king. Walter made arrangements to fight the Prestons in court.

On her way home to Ireland, Elizabeth travelled through Wales, where she suddenly became very ill and died. Two weeks later, Richard Preston sailed the Irish Sea to attend her funeral and drowned during a storm on the journey over. So Walter inherited the castle and all the lands eventually.

The Prestons left behind a daughter, called Elizabeth. Thomas, Walter's son, had died before inheriting, and left behind children. His oldest son was called James Butler.

To bring the two lines of the family together, a marriage was arranged in 1629 between Elizabeth and James, who were second cousins once removed. Elizabeth was 14 and James was 19.

James became the 12th Earl in 1642 and had converted to the Protestant faith while young. Most of the rest of the extended family remained Catholic.

In 1642, he was created the Marquis of Ormonde. It was from this point onwards that the 'e' was added to the title.

Piers Rua. 8th Earl of Ormond. Tomb stone at St Canice's Cathedral

Charles I made James head of his army in Ireland in 1641 and in 1643 he appointed him Lord Lieutenant. However, James was not a popular man in Kilkenny. Up to now, the Butlers had always given important government jobs in Kilkenny to local Catholic merchants. James changed this.

In 1641 a rebellion was started by Irish Catholic gentry, who tried to seize control of the English administration in Ireland to force

111

concessions for the Catholics living under English rule. They also feared invasion by Scottish Covenanters and anti-catholic English Parliament forces.

Some of these men were members of Parliament until the rebellion. As parliament could only be called by the King, they decided to form their own, which they called an 'assembly'. Kilkenny became its home during the 1640s and its supporters called themselves "The Confederate Catholics". Nowadays we refer to it as the "Confederation of Kilkenny".

As Lord Lieutenant, James led the king's army against these rebels, many of whom were related to him.

During this time, England was being torn apart by a civil war. The King and his Parliament differed on how to rule the country and ended up at war with each other.

The Confederates in Kilkenny remained loyal to the king and were fighting for the freedom to practise the Catholic religion.

In January 1649, they were trying to work out a peace deal with the English through James Butler. However, less than two weeks later, the P a r l i a m e n t a r i a n s executed Charles I and James Butler fled to France with Charles's sons.

The Butler family crest with motto which translates as 'As I Find'. From the main gate of Kilkenny Castle

Kilkenny Castle and all the Butler property was confiscated by Parliament. In 1660, Charles II was restored to the throne and James Butler was rewarded. He was created Duke of Ormonde and once more appointed as Lord Lieutenant of Ireland. Kilkenny Castle and most of the land was restored to him.

He set about changing the castle from a medieval fortress to a French style chateau like those he had seen in exile.

He knocked down the houses between Rose Inn Street and the castle, in order to create the Parade. His grandson, another James, followed him as the 2nd Duke after he died and finished the work.

The 2nd Duke's big moment came in the war between James II and William of Orange for the throne of England. In 1688, Catholic King James II, was forced to step down in favour of Prince William of Orange, his Protestant nephew and son-in-law from Holland.

King James' army spent most of the winter of 1689 in Kilkenny Castle. The Duke was not present. He favoured William of Orange. A Catholic cousin, Lord Galmoy, stepped into his place and opportunely lived in the Castle.

The decisive battle in the struggle for the throne was at the river Boyne in 1690. The Duke fought for Prince William, who won this battle.

The Duke rushed to the now vacant Kilkenny Castle to receive William, on his way down to Limerick. William's army made Kilkenny its winter headquarters 1690-91 and then it moved to besiege Limerick.

Duke James was rewarded with the Lord Lieutenancy of Ireland. However, he fell foul of William's successor George I as he favoured a return of the Stuart family to the throne. He fled abroad where he finally died.

His brother Charles had so many titles he was never aware that he had inherited the title and had little interest in Kilkenny. He was legally the last Duke. A caretaker looked after Kilkenny Castle for many years and it became very run down.

In the late 18th century, Walter Butler became the 16th Earl and moved into Kilkenny

Castle, which was in very poor condition at the time.

His son, John became the 17th Earl and married Frances Wandesforde of Castlecomer, also known as Anne. She was a very rich lady as a result of the coalmines and brought a fortune to the Butlers.

Walter and Anne spent her money doing up the castle, planting the Castle Park, rerouting the road away from the castle and building the stables and courtyards across the road – now Kilkenny Design Centre.

Walter and Anne's son, also Walter, inherited in 1795. During his time as 17th Earl, the English Crown decided to buy back the right to the Prisage of Wine that the Butler family had been entitled to since the 12th century. The Crown paid £210,000 for it. This money helped to refurbish the castle and to pay for the lavish lifestyle of the Butlers.

Walter was made 1st Marquess of Ormonde in the Irish peerage. His son, James was a friend of the Prince Regent and was made a Marquess

in the English peerage and also Baron Butler.

During the 19th century, the family carried out major work on Kilkenny Castle. They rebuilt the east wing to house their large collection of pictures. They filled out the west curtain wall to provide more bedrooms.

The succeeding Earls and Marquesses lacked the colour of their forebearers. By the 1930s, the Butlers no longer were able to afford the upkeep of Kilkenny Castle.

In 1935 they decided to sell most of their belongings in the castle and leave. An auction took place in November. It lasted for ten days. One of the days was set aside for selling over 6,000 books from the library. Some of the paintings, tapestries and a large marble table remained.

In 1967, Arthur Butler, the 6th Marquess, sold the castle to a Castle Restoration Committee for £50. In later years it was handed over to the state. Charles Butler, the 25th Earl and the last Marquess of Ormonde, died in 1997 age 98. His successor has not yet been agreed.

Mildred Anne Butler

Painter and Water colourist (1858 – 1941)

Mildred Anne was born in Thomastown at Kilmurry House. While she spent some early years abroad, training as a painter, she spent most of her life at Kilmurry. The family home was a Georgian building surrounded by meadows and a lake, with a beautiful garden. This provided her with a backdrop and material for much of her life's work.

Reproduced by kind permission of An Post ©

Mildred Anne Butler, Threshing

She worked in oils and watercolours and was no amateur. In fact, she was one of Ireland's first professional painters. She was a member of the Royal Academy and her works hang in the Tate Gallery in London, the National Gallery of Ireland, the Hugh Lane Gallery and the Ulster Museum in Belfast. Her paintings regularly appear in auction houses such as Christies and are in great demand.

The main theme of her work was nature and, in addition to her landscapes, she captured scenes in the yards and fields around her home. Some focused on the rivalry between birds, and she captured their personalities which shine through today. She painted in the open air which was unusual at the time.

She died at home in 1941 having stopped painting some time before when arthritis made holding a brush too difficult and painful.

113

John Byrne VC

Soldier VC DCM (1832-1879)

A plaque on the wall in Market Square Castlecomer, honours local son John Byrne, holder of the Victoria Cross.

Aged 22, Byrne took part in the Battle of Inkerman in the Crimean War. Early on 5th November 1854, a huge Russian Army, hidden by fog, attacked the British lines.

Total confusion reigned in the mists. Caught up in this were two hundred men of the 68th (Durham) Light Infantry, fighting for their lives. Charging down hill, they drove back three Russian battalions. Then they were attacked.

With their ammunition gone, the soldiers were forced to retreat and leave their wounded behind. As they fell back and the Russians advanced firing, Private Byrne turned and ran back towards the enemy to rescue a badly wounded soldier, Anthony Harman.

On the 11th May, 1855, still in the Crimea, a large Russian force left Sebastopol and attacked two companies of the 68th Light Infantry. The attack was eventually driven off but only after the most fierce hand to hand fighting. John Byrne struggled in the dark and driving rain with a Russian soldier on the parapet of the trench, before bayoneting him and capturing his musket.

After this second act of bravery he was awarded the Victoria Cross. - "an example of bravery the consequence of which was the speedy repulse of the sortie".

By 1863, now a corporal, he received the Distinguished Conduct Medal fighting Maoris in New Zealand. Sadly, his life outside the army was not as successful.

Leaving as a sergeant after 21 years service, he ended up as a labourer in Wales. In 1879, after a fight with a fellow worker who insulted the Victoria Cross, Byrne shot and wounded his opponent and then went home and took his own life. He was only 47. He is buried in Newport in Wales.

Five other Kilkenny men won the Victoria Cross but Byrne is the only one publicly honoured in his home town so far.

John Clyn

Cleric and Annalist (1286 - 1349)

John Clyn was a Franciscan friar. Born somewhere in Leinster, he was present in the Franciscan friary in Kilkenny 1348, when the Black Death struck.

He is mainly known to us as the author of the Annals of Ireland, which recorded little of the affairs of the order but much about what was happening in the world around him, particularly to Irish knights and gentlemen.

He recorded the fall of the belfry of St. Canice's in 1332 after the Alice Kyteler affair, the paving of the streets in 1334, the erection of the market cross in 1335 and the building of the bell tower of St. Mary's 1343.

His eye witness accounts of the effects of the Black Death are what he is chiefly remembered for. He records the pilgrimages which people made to local holy sites, which sadly only helped speed up the transmission of the disease. He lists the numbers of dead reported in many parts of Ireland.

Towards the end of his writing he records the death of the people and clergy in the local community as the

disease came closer to him and his community.

Clyn eventually fell victim to the plague and his final entry echoes the sense of despair felt by many dying at such a time. It also hints at the feeling that the Apocalypse or World's End had eventually come.

"So that notable deeds should not perish with time, and be lost from the memory of future generations, I, seeing these many ills, and that the whole world encompassed by evil, waiting among the dead for death to come, have committed to writing what I have truly heard and examined; and so that the writing does not perish with the writer, or the work fail with the workman, I leave parchment for continuing the work, in case anyone should still be alive in the future and any son of Adam can escape this pestilence and continue the work thus begun."

Here his writing breaks off and is followed by a note in another hand: *"Here it seems, the Author died."*

**The Black Death.
1345-50**

Plagues were not unknown to medieval people. However, the Black Death was the most devastating, killing between 70 and 200 million people in Europe.

Fleas, travelling from Asia, carried by black rats, brought the infection which killed 30%-60% of the population of Europe.

Sufferers showed strange black egg-sized swellings in the armpits and groin. These oozed blood and pus and were followed by spreading boils and black blotches on the skin from internal bleeding.

The sick suffered severe pain and died quickly within five days of the first symptoms.

As the disease spread, symptoms of continuous fever appeared. These were accompanied by spitting blood and horrible swellings or buboes. By now, victims coughed and sweated heavily and death came quickly, within three days or less, sometimes in 24 hours.

In both types everything that issued from the body- breath, sweat, blood from the buboes and lungs, bloody urine, and blood-blackened excrement, smelled foul.

Depression and despair accompanied the physical symptoms as neither the cause nor the cure was known.

Ellen Odette Bischoffsheim - Lady Desart

Philanthropist & Senator. (1857 – 1933)

Daughter of a Jewish Dutch banker, Henry Bischoffsheim, Ellen married William Cuffe from Kilkenny in 1881. She was his second wife. A writer, who wrote thrillers, William was the 4th Lord Desart and so she became Lady Desart. They lived in the family ancestral home in Cuffesgrange, west of the city on their 8,000 acre estate. However, the Irish Land wars started three years later and they moved to live in England. William died in 1898.

In 1908, her father died leaving her £15 million, a colossal fortune at that time. Still living in England, Lady Ellen maintained her links with Kilkenny and on the death of her brother-in-law, who had been mayor of Kilkenny, she moved to a new home at Aut Even

on the north side of the city.

Lady Ellen decided to use her fortune to the benefit of others. She invested the money in various projects in the city and abroad. In Kilkenny, she paid for the building of Kilkenny City Library, on the quay side opposite the footbridge, which bears her name, across the Nore. She also built a hospital, which still serves the city, a theatre, sadly now gone, woollen mills and a village for the workers amongst other works. She also invested in the Gaelic revival locally, supporting interest in the Irish language and became president of the local Gaelic league at a time when Irish Nationalism was coming to the fore.

In 1923, she was one of the first women to be appointed senator in the new Irish Senate and the first Jewish woman to receive this honour in the world. She remained a senator until her death.

Her last great gift was made in 1933 when she used part of her remaining fortune to rescue 20,000 Jewish children. Paying for their train and boat from Berlin to Tel Aviv, she saved them from the threat posed by Nazi race policy.

On her death, she was buried in Falmouth in England beside her late husband.

James Hoban

Architect (1758 - 1831)

An Irish architect whose most famous achievement was the design of the White House in Washington USA, James Hoban was born in a thatched cottage on the estate of the Cuffe family, Earls of Desart in the townsland of Reiske, near Callan. A carpenter and wheelwright he advanced to become the architect of one of the world's most iconic buildings.

His father worked as a tenant farmer or an estate labourer on the Desart Court lands. James was educated at the estate school. He must have shown a talent for drawing because Lord Ottway Cuffe helped him attended the Dublin Society's Drawing School.

He received the Duke of Leinster's medal for drawings of "Brackets, Stairs, and Roofs". Heady stuff. With this in his pocket, James became an apprentice to the Cork-born architect Thomas Ivory, the headmaster of the Dublin Society School from 1759 to 1786.

By 1785, he had moved to America where he placed the following snappy ad in a Philadelphia newspaper:

"Any gentleman, who wishes to build in an elegant style, may hear of a person properly calculated for that purpose who can execute the Joining and Carpenter's business in the modern taste.   James Hoban."

Two years later, he moved to Charleston, South Carolina, with his two brothers, where he began to build his reputation and make connections. He worked on a number of public buildings throughout the state and was in demand through the plantations of the region.

A national competition was held to pick the designer of both the President's House and the Capitol building. President Washington sought out Hoban, conferred with him, and quickly selected the architect's proposed design for the President's House in July 1792.

His design for the presidential mansion is said to be modelled on the design of Leinster House, Dublin, originally the home of the Duke of Leinster and now the seat of Dail Eireann.

The building has changed many times in its existence but it still remains the house that Hoban built. In fact he is responsible for some of the changes which he carried out for three more presidents.

By 1798, Hoban became superintendent of all Washington's public works, directing the construction of many of the city's prominent buildings of the time.

James Hoban died in 1831, a rich and highly respected man… who started life in a thatched cottage near Callan.

Hoban was honoured in the first joint issue of a stamp by An Post, which issued the stamp on the right in 1981 jointly with the U.S. Postal Service, to commemorate the 250th anniversary of his death. The stamp shows the White House as Hoban first built it.

Reproduced by kind permission of An Post ©

Thomas Kilroy

Playwright and novelist. (1934 - 2023)

Thomas Kilroy was born in Green Street, Callan. His father was the local Garda sergeant and was an IRA veteran. From such modest beginnings he has become one of Ireland's most important living dramatists.

His only novel, The Big Chapel, based on events in 19th century Callan, was nominated for a Booker prize in 1971.

However, it was in the theatre, through his work with the Field day Theatre Company and the Abbey Theatre, that his main impact has been seen.

Through such works as The Death and Resurrection of Mr Roche, The Madam MacAdam Travelling Theatre and Talbot's Box in the 1970s to Christ Deliver Us! in 2010, he remains a leading voice in Irish theatre.

Right: Cover of Pan edition of the Big Chapel published in 1973.

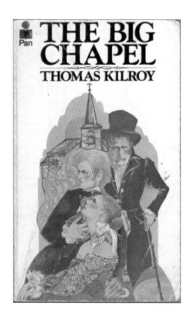

Alice Kyteler

Business woman & Witch (1280 - ?)

Alice Kyteler was born in Kieran St, where her father carried on a banking business. The family had come to Ireland after the Norman conquest of 1169.

After his death, the young Alice inherited his property. In 1299, she married one of her father's former associates, William Outlawe, who was also a highly successful banker.

William was twenty years older than Alice. They had a son called William Junior. In time, Dame Alice decided to build an addition to their house extending it and developing it as an inn.

She was a good looking woman, who could manipulate men. Soon Kyteler's Inn became the rendezvous for wealthy men, both young and not so young, who vied for the attentions of the fascinating Dame Alice.

Rumours started of Alice practicing Satanic rites and, when William died suddenly in 1302, it was said that he had found terrible things in a jar in the house. It contained evil smelling entrails of cocks and eyes of ravens, horrible worms and sprigs of deadly night-shade, dead men's hair and fragments of unbaptised babies, cooked in a pot made from the skull of a beheaded thief. Shocking stuff. Poor widowed Alice inherited all his property to add to her own.

Months later, Dame Alice married another banker from Callan, named Adam Le Blont and they had a daughter. In 1310, Le Blont died after a 'drinking spree'. Alice came into her third inheritance.

Dame Alice was fast becoming the wealthiest woman in Kilkenny. Envied, she was also seen as the most wicked.

She had gathered a group of young women around her to help with the running of the Inn, which was Kilkenny's busiest. But rumours were that they were also involved with Alice in demonology.

One in particular, pleased her more than all

the others, was Petronella de Meath. She would eventually pay the ultimate price for Alice's friendship.

Dame Alice married her third husband, Richard De Valle in 1311. He was a wealthy landlord, who owned extensive properties in and around Clonmel. Richard also left this earth unexpectedly, after a sumptuous supper. Alice inherited for a fourth time and was now one of the wealthiest people in Leinster.

Meanwhile, she was suspected of becoming more deeply involved with Satan. It was said that her favourite devil was Robin, Son of Artisson, who was also her lover. W.B. Yeats referred to their relationship in his poem 'N i n e t e e n Hundred and Nineteen'.

It was also said that she led n i g h t l y gatherings at the crossroads, where living animals were cruelly dismembered and offered to demons.

In spite of the rumours, Dame Alice managed to find a fourth husband around 1320. The happy man was John Le Poer, a regular at the inn.

By 1323, poor John found himself suffering from many different sicknesses. Although he was only middle-aged, he became feeble and slow. His hair fell out in patches and what remained turned silvery grey and his finger nails fell out. Maybe he was too good a customer of the Inn.

Fearing that it was Dame Alice's doing, just before he died in 1324, he went to the Friars at St Francis's Abbey for help. They contacted Richard de Ledrede, Bishop of Ossory, giving him their full account of Dame Alice's coven of witches and her involvement in the deaths of her four husbands, amongst other things.

The timing of the claim was fortuitous as the Catholic Church had begun its medieval obsession with witchcraft. Alice was in deep trouble.

Richard de Ledrede made every attempt to have this coven arrested but was hindered by Alice's influential network of friends, including the brother of her first husband William, who was now Chancellor of all Ireland.

The Bishop did, however, hold an inquisition in 1324, at which she was found guilty of witchcraft and magic, of heresy and of having sacrificed to demons. She was excommunicated.

In those medieval times, for one to be found guilty of witchcraft was a most serious offence, which carried the sentence of death.

Unexpectedly, Alice turned the tables and it was the Bishop who was jailed for 17 days on bread and water. It took a visit by the Lord Chief Justice, to release Ledrede, and he confirmed the sentence against Alice and her followers, starting her downfall.

Alice's son William, who was one of those found guilty, escaped relatively lightly, being ordered to hear three masses a day for a year and to feed the poor. He also had to pay for a new roof for the cathedral, which later fell in.

Dame Alice and her other followers were condemned to be whipped through the streets, tied at the back of a horse and cart, after which Alice, as chief priestess and instigator, would be burned at the stake.

But, by the political power of her former brother-in-law, her escape to London was organised. Her guards were knocked out and Dame Alice was released from the dungeons beneath Kilkenny Castle. She fled in the night, never again to set foot in her native Kilkenny.

Poor Petronella de Meath wasn't so lucky. To satisfy the blood thirsty mob that had gathered around the huge pyre in front of the old Tholsel, in the centre of Kilkenny, Petronella would be sacrificed in place of Alice.

Already suffering from the whippings, she confessed to everything she was charged with. She told them it was Dame Alice made her deny that Jesus Christ was the son of God; also that she had called up demons and worshipped them. Her pleas for mercy went unheard.

Petronella was burned alive at the stake before the mob, as she screamed in vain for Alice to come to her aid.

It was the first witch burning in Medieval Europe.

Alice Kyteler's home is today a popular pub on Kieran St.

Tony O'Malley

Artist (1913 - 2003)

Born in Callan in 1913, Tony O'Malley drew and painted as a child but a career in banking in the 1930s seemed a safer way of life. However, he suffered from tuberculosis like many at that time and while convalescing he began painting in earnest and was self taught. He returned to banking for a period but by 1951 he was exhibiting his work.

In 1955 he holidayed in St. Ives in

Arrieta - Orzola (Lanzarote) 1988 Oil on board as used in An Post stamp issued 1993. The original painting sold in 2004 for €45,000. Reproduced by kind permission of An Post ©

Cornwall, then an important centre of abstract art. After further trips in the next two years convinced him he had a future as a painter, Tony retired from the bank in his 40s to paint full time. In 1950s Ireland this was a very courageous move. Prompted by frustration at the indifference shown in Ireland to his work, he moved to and settled in St Ives in 1960, where he married in 1973 at the age of 50. In the 70s he spent time in the Bahamas and in Callan, finally returning to Callan in 1990 for good.

O'Malley has been widely recognized as one of the leading Irish painters of his time, with major exhibitions throughout Ireland and the United States. In 1999 he was the recipient of the Glen Dimplex Award for a Sustained Contribution to the Visual Arts in Ireland. He was a member of Aosdána and was elected Saoi in 1993.

Regarded as one of Ireland's leading painters, he died in 2003. His work is held in many public and private collections in Ireland and throughout the world. The city's Butler Gallery has a permanent exhibition of his work.

Blessed Edmund Ignatius Rice

Educator and missionary (1762 – 1844)

Edmund was Callan born and bred. He was raised in a difficult time for Catholics in Ireland, when the Penal Laws restricted the practicing of religion, access to education and exclusion from public office.

Young Edmund could not attend a formal school and was educated at a 'hedge school'. This was a form of clandestine school. In Edmund's case he was educated by a friar in a neighbours house.

The Rice family were not poor and at aged 17 he was apprenticed to his uncle, a merchant in Waterford.

When aged 23, he married but wedded life did not last long and his wife died four years later in an accident. Before she died, she gave birth to their daughter Mary, who was disabled.

Edmund worked hard at his business and in charitable work in his spare time. Waterford had many poor at the time and in 1802, he decided to start his own form of hedge school in stables around the town.

Friends told Mr. Rice that he was wasting his time and even doing damage by educating the poor. He ignored them. However, he found that the teachers could not handle the pupils.

Frustrated with this, he sold his thriving business and set out to train his own teachers, who would teach the children free of charge.

The school started to thrive and he opened another. He was joined by two more Callan men and others started to join them to form a congregation devoted to God and teaching.

Using his family connections in the world of commerce he obtained the licences needed to operate Catholic schools under the laws of the time.

Edmund took religious vows and in time, as his school network grew, he founded the Christian Brothers and the Presentation Brothers as two separate congregations. Both remained dedicated to teaching, especially the poor and marginalised, using the methods set down by their founder.

The Christian Brothers in particular were seen as strong supporters of Irish nationalism, the Irish language and Irish sport.

In the intervening two centuries, both organisations have been leading educators to all levels of society in Ireland. Each has also become an international organisation, with houses in the UK, USA and Australia, as well as missions in many countries in Africa and South America.

Edmund died in 1844 and his remains are in Mount Sion, his first school, in Waterford. Since 1911, efforts were made to introduce his cause to sainthood and in October 1996 he was beatified and his official feast day is May 5th.

A statue of him stands on the high end of the Callan town, appropriately opposite the local church.

Visit Westcourt in Callan where the home he came from still exists and has been lovingly restored. It is beside a monastery founded by the Christian Brother Order that he founded and carries on his work.

Edmund Rice commemorated in 1994 on the 150th anniversary of his death.

Reproduced by kind permission of An Post ©

Red Rum

Racehorse (1965 – 1995)

Arguably the most famous European racehorse of all time was Kilkenny born Red Rum. He was bred at Rossenarra stud in Kells by Martyn Mc Enery. The horse got his name his name by taking the last three letters of the names of his dam Mared and his sire Quorum respectively.

He was bred to be a sprinter but he won his greatest races over the longest distance, four miles and four furlongs.

He was sold as a yearling from the Rossenarra yard and began running in cheap races as a sprinter and passed from training yard to training yard. In 1969/70 he ran fourteen races over hurdles and won none.

His career changed when, in 1972, Ginger McCain, a car dealer from the South of England bought him for a client and trained him on the sands at Southport. The sea water must have helped because the legend began from then.

In 1973, Red Rum won his first Grand National in a record time, catching the leader Crisp who had a 15 length lead coming over the last fence. It is regarded as one of the greatest Grand Nationals in history. A year later, Red Rum retained his title carrying 12 stone.

That seemed to be it for Red Rum. He came second in 1975 and 1976. But he had one last shot left in his locker and in 1977 he thundered to his third Grand National win.

The day before the 1978 race he suffered a hairline fracture and the decision was made to let him retire. His record of three wins and two second places is never likely to be equalled

However, he didn't fade into obscurity. Now a celebrity, Red Rum made personal appearances opening supermarkets and once, a roller coaster.

Each year, he led the Grand National parade. Posters, mugs, paintings, jigsaws, plates and models sold well with his image. In 1977, he appeared as a studio guest at the BBC Sports Personality of the Year award.

Red Rum died on 18 October 1995, aged 30. His death made the front pages of national newspapers. He is buried at the winning post of the Aintree Racecourse.

James Stephens

Republican and Fenian (1825 - 1901)

Founder in 1858 of a revolutionary organisation, later known as Irish Republican Brotherhood (I.R.B.), James Stephens can lay a strong claim to be the grandfather of Irish Independence.

He was born and raised at Lilac Cottage, Blackmill Street, Kilkenny. The original cottage no longer stands but a plaque on the wall of its replacement marks where he started life.

Although having nationalist tendencies, it wasn't until 1848, when revolution swept Europe starting with barricades in Paris in February, that Stephens publicly declared his beliefs at a public meeting in Kilkenny.

Soon afterwards he was ready to turn words to action, when he took part in the Young Irelander's uprising of 1848 at Ballingarry, Co Tipperary.

The brief revolt was quickly put down and the leaders arrested. The local newspapers reported on the death and funeral of Stephens but it was a ruse. He lived.

He fled to France were he stayed for the next seven years. There he set himself three aims; to keep alive, pursue knowledge, and master the technique of conspiracy. Paris was the best place in Europe to learn conspiracy at that time.

In 1856 he returned to Ireland and began what he called his "three thousand mile walk", meeting fellow revolutionaries, networking and organising.

In 1857, he formed the Irish Republican Brotherhood, a secret organisation, with him as its leader. I.R.B. members were known as Fenians.

The following year he sailed to New York, where he raised awareness of Irish Republican unrest, organised and fund raised. While there he kept a diary which showed the infighting and divisiveness he had to overcome to reach his goal.

Returning to Ireland, he started a newspaper, the Irish People, to promote the revolutionary cause.

In 1865, he tried to start a rising but it failed and later that year was arrested for conspiracy but he managed to escape and fled to New York. His paper was suppressed.

His influence was on the wane. For the next 20 years he moved between New York and Europe. In 1891, he was allowed to return to Ireland where he lived a life of seclusion.

Many of the members of his organisation formed the leadership of the Irish Volunteers in the 1916 insurrection, which lit the fuse for eventual Irish Freedom soon afterwards.

Stephens didn't live to see his dream come true, dying peacefully in Dublin in 1901.

He is still remembered in Kilkenny where a senior hurling club in the city is named after him.

Down the Family Trees

Not every person who left Kilkenny made a world wide impact. In some cases, it took a generation or two or three. The following are two descendants who made it.

Walt Disney

Cartoonist and Filmmaker. (1901 -1966)

In 1801, Arundel Elias Disney, great grandfather of Walt Disney was born near Gowran, Co Kilkenny in 1801. He was a descendant of Robert d'Isigny, who settled in England with William the Conqueror in 1066. Isigny is a town in Brittany and the Disneys came with Cromwell's Army in the 17th century.

In 1834 Arundel emigrated to America and then to Canada. In 1859, his son Kepple was born.

As he grew older, Kepple moved to California to dig for gold, unsuccessfully. In 1884, Arundel and Kepple and their families moved to a farm in Ellis, Kansas, but in time Kepple moved on trying various jobs as he moved around America. He married in 1888 and his fourth child, Walt, was born in Chicago in 1901.

Asa Griggs Candler

Businessman (1851 - 1929)

In 1888, Asa Griggs Candler bought the formula to a syrupy patent medicine from John Pemberton of Georgia, USA for €500.

Through aggressive and imaginative marketing and a change of name to Coca Cola, he created one of the world's most recognisable brands, drunk in every country in the world.

Asa's father was Samuel Candler. Samuel's grandfather, William, emigrated to America from Callan, Co Kilkenny in the 1730s.

The family's roots in Callan were so important, that Asa's mansion which still stands today in Atlanta, is called Callan Castle.

His son Charles, built a later mansion which he names Callanwolde, (Callan Wood) keeping the link alive.

If you are interested in finding out about more of Kilkenny's interesting people, famous and unknown, rich and poor, villain or saint, please look for a copy of 99 *Lives - Kilkenny Connections* also by Donal Cadogan

ÉIRE
78c

KILKENNY ÇAT • CAT CHILL CHAINNIGH
2007

Essence of Kilkenny

What Makes a Kilkenny Person?

The spirit and soul of a community is expressed in what its people hold dear and of value; in how they show their individuality from the world around and in what they create to express their inner spirit and to reflect their place.

Kilkenny is no different. To many, the name Kilkenny will immediately call to mind hurling, beer, cats, black and amber, the Marble City, but it is much more than this. It is local craft and design, literature and writers, Irish music in the pubs, Michelin starred restaurants, modern art.

The city hosts one of the country's oldest Arts Festivals each year. There are also festivals which cater for comedy, music, books, economics, racing in wellington boots and fighting with conkers; an eclectic mix not to be found anywhere else.

The county is filled with creativity. An organised craft trail has been designated to highlight the breadth of disciplines being pursued in the community. Much of this stems from the arrival of the Craft Council in the 1960s with the set up of the Kilkenny Design Workshops. This stimulated the craft scene and the seeds planted flourish after the Workshops themselves have closed.

Kilkenny inspires in many other ways. Cartoon Saloon, from the city, was nominated for Oscars for four full length animated movies. *The Secret of Kells, Song of the Sea, The Breadwinner* and *Wolfwalkers*. The last one was set in 1650's Kilkenny and gives a feel for what the city felt like under rule of Oliver Cromwell.

A single rose found on a walk in the garden in Jenkinstown in 1805, inspired poet and singer Thomas Moore to write *'The Last Rose of Summer'*. It was popular in drawing rooms across Europe and referenced in works by Beethoven, Mendelssohn and the Grateful Dead.

It appears in a story by Jules Verne, 'The Moonstone' by Wilkie Collins and 'Ulysses' by James Joyce. It has even been used in the game 'Endless Ocean 2'.

So what follows is a scrap book of sorts. It will try to explain some of what makes people in Kilkenny into Kilkenny People.

Overleaf: Kilkenny Cat from the Celtic Cat series of stamps produced by cartoonist Martyn Turner for An Post in 2007.
Reproduced by kind permission of An Post ©

Kilkenny Cats

There once were two cats from Kilkenny
Each thought there was one cat too many.
So they fought and they fit
And they scratched and they bit
And instead of two cats, there ain't any!

Kilkenny people are traditionally known as The Cats. The historic reason for this is open to argument. So let's argue.

Version 1. (The Real Story?). Over the centuries, soldiers have been stationed in Kilkenny, which is in a strategic location. At one stage, either during the revolution of 1798 or possibly that of 1803, the legend was born (or was it?).

To relieve the boredom in barracks, the soldiers here at the time would tie two cats together by their tails, hang them over a washing line and leave them to fight. You had to make your own entertainment in those days.

One day an officer heard the awful noise and the look-out man failed to give warning of his approach in time. Hurriedly, a soldier cut off the cats' tails to let them escape, but wasn't able to hide the evidence of the two tails left behind. The officer was told that two cats had been fighting each other so savagely it had proved impossible to separate them. In fact they fought so desperately that they had eaten each other up, with the exception of their tails.

The moral of the story is that Kilkenny people will fight to the end.

Version 2. (Ancient Legend). Once upon a time, long, long ago, there was a battle near Kilkenny, between a thousand cats from the city and a thousand cats that had gathered from all over Ireland. This left the field of battle covered with dead moggies, they having fought so viciously that they had all killed each other.

This may be based on historical disagreements at the time between the people of the Kilkenny area and other parts of Ireland. Now we are pussy cats and welcome every one.

Version 3. (The Historical Context). In the fourteenth century, Kilkenny was divided into two townships called Irishtown and Hightown, a common situation in a country occupied for so long by the English. For religious, cultural and political reasons there were deep divisions between the two groups.

These were made worse because the rights and duties of the two townships hadn't been made clear by statute. This led to three centuries of dispute between the rival municipal bodies that ended in beggaring both sides. Thus the people from the different parts of Kilkenny city were always at each others throats.

Regardless of where the phrase started, two people furiously fighting with each other are sometimes described as fighting like Kilkenny cats.

Which ever story is true, being a Cat has become a mark of honour for the people of Kilkenny.

The Rose of Mooncoin

Every county in Ireland has a maudlin ballad which serves as an anthem to bring its natives together, where ever they may be around the world. Kilkenny is no different. Its ballad of choice is the Rose of Mooncoin. It is most often sung where lonely immigrants gather and each September as the county hurling team tries to win another All Ireland title.

Written in the 19th century by a Watt Murphy, a schoolteacher in Mooncoin in the south of the county, it is in memory of his lost love, Molly. Molly was the pet name of Elizabeth who at 20 years old, was 36 years younger than love struck Watt. Elizabeth's father, the local vicar, disapproved of the match because of the age gap and because Molly was Protestant and Watt a Catholic. It was not a suitable match and he sent her away. Poor Watt picked up his pen and wrote the words of loss and longing, which have been adopted as an anthem to bring Kilkenny people together around the world.

The Rose of Mooncoin

How sweet is to roam by the sunny Suir stream
And hear the doves coo 'neath the morning sunbeam
Where the thrush and the robin their sweet notes entwine
On the banks of the Suir that flows down by Mooncoin.

Flow on, lovely river, flow gently along
By your waters so sweet sounds the lark's merry song
On your green banks I wander where first I did join
With you, lovely Molly, the rose of Mooncoin.

Oh Molly, dear Molly, it breaks my fond heart
To know that we two forever must part
I'll think of you Molly while sun and moon shine
On the banks of the Suir that flows down by Mooncoin.

Then here's to the Suir with its valley so fair
As oft times we wandered in the cool morning air
Where the roses are blooming and lilies entwine
On the banks of the Suir that flows down by Mooncoin.

Flow on, lovely river, flow gently along
By your waters so sweet sounds the lark's merry song
On your green banks I wander where first I did join
With you, lovely Molly, the rose of Mooncoin.

Hurling *(Iománaíocht)*

The game of hurling is synonymous with Kilkenny. On a summer's day, teenagers can be found on the Parade or in the Castle Park practicing the game. Even during the school year, many children carry their hurley to school and home, even if there is no training or game on the day.

Hurling is Ireland's oldest field game. First mention is almost 3,000 years ago when the Firbolg, early inhabitants of the island, played the Tuath de Danann in a match. The Firbolg won but there is no record of the score.

History's most famous hurler was Setanta. His name was later changed to Cuchulainn after he killed the hound of Cualann with one shot from his hurley and ball.

The ancient Brehon laws also mentioned hurling, listing the compensation to be paid for any one injured or killed by a hurley or ball. It ruled that the son of the chieftain was allowed have a band of gold around his hurley.

After the arrival of the Normans, they gradually began to become integrated with the native Irish. One of the signs of integration of the invaders was their joining in the game. To prevent this integration the Statutes of Kilkenny were passed and these included a ban on the playing of the game.

It remained strong however. Gaelic chieftains and English landlords kept teams of paid hurlers, an early example of the professional sportsman.

By the end of the 18th Century, revolution was afoot across Europe and in 1798, a rising of the native Irish was brutally suppressed by the English and the sometimes cosy relationship between landlord and tenant ended.

In the early part of the 19th century, hurling had become a dangerous game and partisan followers broke up many a match with fierce fighting. The game lost its attraction for many.

Interest died off and by 1860, the game had been supplanted by cricket with almost every town in Ireland having its own club.

Kilkenny was not immune and by the end of the 19th century there were more cricket clubs than hurling clubs in the county.

In 1884, the Gaelic Athletic Association (GAA) was formed to promote the game nationally, together with Gaelic Football. Rules were agreed.

Early teams fielded 21 players. This was later reduced to 17 and finally to 15 players, which is the modern team.

In early games, the most number of goals scored won a match and points were only considered if there was a draw. Later this changed to counting both with a goal worth five points.

Eventually this changed to 3 points as it is today.

While it remains a physical game, wrestling opponents to the ground was banned in 1886, was even more robust.

19th century society could not have considered a sport like hurling as suitable for women. It took until 1903 for the experiment to start.

Early games were played in ground length skirts and it was a foul for a player deliberately to stop a sliotar in the folds her skirt.

The women's game, called Camogie, developed over the years and is now played in any club where hurling is played. Like Gaelic Football, the other great national game, hurling and camogie are amateur sports.

Under the GAA system, clubs are

predominately based on the local parishes. Every Kilkenny child aspires to play for his or her club and for the county. This creates ties that start in childhood and hold communities together over the years.

The county colours are vertical black & amber stripes and worn with pride by fans from every age and social group.

The All Ireland Championship is played throughout each summer between county teams and ends in the All Ireland final in Croke Park in Dublin on the first Sunday each September. For hurlers it is the World Cup and World Series wrapped in one.

Kilkenny has always been strong in the game but, since the last few years of the 20th century, the team has achieved levels never seen before in the game and the county has more titles than any other.

Near final day, the city can become a sea of black and amber with some suburbs going to great lengths to decorate every inch of house and garden. Should the team win, the homecoming can bring together almost every living person in the county to acclaim the return of the All Ireland trophy.

HOW TO PLAY

Hurling is played with a stick called a hurley, or hurl, and a ball called a sliotar (shlith-her).

The hurley is made of ash timber, taken from the base of the tree. One tree can make about 12 hurleys.

Using about 1.2m from where the trunk and root meets, the timber is harvested in November or December when sap flow is at its lowest. The timber is left to dry for 9 months.

Wood from the joining of the root and stem gives a curved grain, which flows along the bas (or toe) of the stick. This makes it strong and flexible. A metal strip is added to prevent splitting.

The sliotar is smaller in size than a baseball but slightly larger than a tennis ball, Traditionally, it is made with a cork centre, wrapped in yarn. The core is then dipped in latex and, when dried, this is stitched inside two pieces of leather The seams are blackened to make the seam waterproof, giving the sliotar its distinctive appearance.

Teams are 15 a-side, with a goalkeeper and 14 outfield players. All players wear helmets to prevent injury. A player may strike the ball on the ground, or in the air with the hurley.

Unlike field hockey, the sliotar can be picked up to the hand using the hurley and it can be carried for not more than four steps this way. After those steps the sliotar can be bounced on the hurley and back to the hand, but a player is forbidden to catch the ball more than twice.

To get around this, one of the skills is running at speed with the sliotar balanced on the hurley, while an opponent tries to knock it off.

The pitch is almost twice the size of a soccer pitch and to get from one end to the other quickly, the sliotar is struck through the air with the hurl. A good player can strike a ball 100m. That is 23 car lengths. The ball can travel at 160 kph (100 mph).

Players beneath a falling sliotar will leap to great heights to catch it ahead of an opponent, who may be using a hurley to do the same thing. It requires great bravery and skill to do this.

To score, the sliotar must be struck over the crossbar and between the posts for a point or under the crossbar and into the net for a goal, the latter being the equivalent of three points.

Games usually last 60 minutes with a half time break, although All Ireland championship games are 70 minutes long.

Fielding a high ball. No place for the weak.

Black &

Depending on the time of the year Kilkenny can appear to be a city of only two colours; black and amber. These are the colours of the county GAA sides and particularly the hurling team.

Tullaroan was the first Kilkenny team to wear the famous black and amber colours. In 1886, after winning the first-ever county championship in Kilkenny they held a fund-raising event in Tullaroan to provide the team with a playing strip.

After intensive debate and consultations the club chose the black and amber stripes as the design for the jerseys that they would wear against Limerick that August.

Since then, the colours have become the mark by which Kilkenny people identify themselves throughout the world.

Amber

Right: Striking the sliotar, while under pressure. A crucial skill.

129

Running at speed with the sliotar using only the hurley.   *Photos: Courtesy of Kilkenny G.A.A.*

Marble City

The city of Kilkenny is often referred to as "The Marble City". Marble is a form of limestone capable of taking a polish. Such limestone can be found close to the city and was mined in an area now known as the Black Quarry, due to the deep jet black colour of the final product.

With easy access to this stone, it was used amongst other things to pave the footpaths of the city streets. With wear, the limestone took on a sheen which, when wet, glistened.

On a wet night in the light of flickering torches or early street lights, the shiny paths must have been a tricky prospect. To a visitor, the shiny paths must have seemed to be paved with marble.

Large blocks of stone were cut from the quarry and brought on horse-drawn carts to the nearby river where they were loaded onto small barges and brought 3km down river to stone mills, where it was cut and shaped.

A weir on the river supplied the water to drive the 4m steel band saws which cut the blocks into the sizes needed and rail tracks were eventually set down to help move the heavy stone.

The Black Quarry is known to have been in use since the 17th century, but fell into disuse as fashions changed and closed in the 1920s. It was filled-in in the 1970's.

A cliff face still remains exposed and can be seen from the Bennettsbridge road beside the service station. Hard as it might seem today, this quarry was once a tourist attraction that people came specifically to see.

Kilkenny Black Marble was in great demand in 19th century for public buildings and stately homes across the UK, with many having stone from Kilkenny decorating the floors and fireplaces. The marble is still produced in small quantities from a quarry near Gowran. Kilkenny city has local limestone on many of its public buildings and you will see the shine appear where the stone has started to wear.

Visitors will see it in abundance in St Canice's Cathedral and the Black Abbey. A good example would be the face of St Canice in his statue on Irishtown (page 4t), where the hands of many tourists have brought a shine to his cheeks and chin.

Kilkenny

A - Z

Tired of Sightseeing?

After you have had your fill of seeing the sights, listening to the tour guide or relaxing while the world passes you by, you may reach the stage where you want to shake out those legs and do something.

The following pages will give you a choice of activities. Try something new or enjoy something you already know is fun.

For most of the activities, you can just phone ahead and book. Very few require equipment which you need to have brought with you. So you can hire the clubs, the pony, the target rifle, the bows and arrows or the bike.

It doesn't have to be a strenuous task. You can walk through a wood, stroll through a garden, ramble by a river or just stand in the stream and wait for a catch.

For the younger visitors there is also a list of things which might interest them, from picnics to farm visits.

Not everyone wants physical activity on a break. The following pages also have suggestions for those whose idea of an activity is to shop.

However, shopping is one activity where the hunt can be as rewarding as finding what you looked for and an unexpected find is the best part of the day. So the list is not extensive and you can enjoy the chase in your own way.

Finally, at the end there is a selection of places you can eat around the city. It only a sample and there is something for everyone. Be sure to check out Kilkenny's two Michelin starred restaurants.

Activity Centres

Countryside Leisure Activity Centre caters for shooters and archers. As well as shooting at an indoor target with rifles, this is your chance to go outdoors and try clay pigeon shooting or long bow archery. An over 18 age limit applies.

The centre is located on the Glendine Road, north of the city. To get there travel out the Castlecomer Road to the turning for Kilkenny Golf Club, opposite the Glendine Inn. Past the Golf Club, almost 1 km out this road there is a turnoff to the right and the Centre is 750m up this way. It is advisable to phone ahead to make a booking and it is great for groups.

Web: www.countrysideleisureactivitycentre.ie. Tel: 056-7761791.

Kilkenny's Activity Centre is next to the Orchard House bar on the New Orchard Road. It is home to the city's paintball zone It is surrounded by trees and hedgerows, great for hiding behind or crawling through. There is also a five acre assault course. Although it may not cause a heart attack to a team of Irish Rangers, it will challenge an amateur. The swamp will take you if you are not careful.

Splatball, a low velocity alternative for kids, is also available here as well as giant darts and bubble football, where the players are wrapped in giant bubbles. A handy bar and restaurant are next door to help recovery. To get there, turn towards town on the New Orchard roundabout (junction 9) on the Ring Road. The centre is on your right after 300 metres.

Check out www.kilkennyactivitycentre.ie or Tel: 086-2611567.

Finally, the Discovery Park in Castlecomer provides the adrenaline rush of a zip wire trip across a lake, a rope walk high amongst the trees or the satisfaction of conquering the climbing wall. Throw in axe throwing, archery and mountain biking and you can't miss.

Web: www.discoverypark.ie Tel: 056-4440707.

Previous page: Strolling along the canal walk between the Castle Park and the River Nore.

Angling

The main fishing on the Nore is from the city down to Inistioge, which is the limit of the reach of the tide. It is basically a limestone river with very rich fly life and weirs are a feature. The banks are high in places which can make fishing difficult. Some stretches are fly only and most of the rights are either exercised by private owners or leased to angling clubs.

There is good fishing there for salmon and brown trout. They are in season from March 17th to 30th September each year. The Nore provides for catch and release all year round and is open for angling from 12th May. The Anglers Association has fishing rights over much of the river and welcomes visitors. Day permits are available from the Club House Hotel in the city Tel: 056-7721994.

Fishing for trout and salmon is also one of the activities at Jerpoint Park (Page 88). Rods are available to hire. Tel: 086-6061449.

The River Barrow at Graiguenamanagh is good water for Pike. At Tinnahinch, on the Carlow side of the bridge, rudd, perch and bream can be found in good numbers. At Clashganny Lock, 5k north of the town, is a good stretch for specimen fish. Bream can be plentiful in the fast water of the weir. Anglers should note the game fishing stretches and observe local club regulations.

There is fishing tackle available at Mick Doyle's Bar on Main St. Graiguenamanagh and he can offer angling advice, the best stands for fishing, contact numbers for angling guides, etc.

For the novice, Castlecomer Demesne provides a gentle introduction to the sport of fishing. The focus of the park is two lakes stocked with rainbow trout. You can try bait fishing in one or the more artistic fly fishing in the other. Rods can be rented and bait and flies can be bought on site. If you book in advance, you can even have lessons from a hardened angler.
Web: www.discoverypark.ie. Tel: 056-4440707.

Art Gallery

The Butler Gallery was established in Kilkenny in 1943 and it focuses on contemporary visual art. Its programme is committed to promoting Irish artists but has regularly brought thoughtful and provocative works from abroad. It has a permanent exhibition of the work of Kilkenny artist, Tony O'Malley as well as a collection of works by major Irish artists from the Butler Collection. It is located just off Johns Quay.
Monday: closed (except Bank Holidays when Sunday hours apply). Tuesday-Saturday: 10.00–17.00. Thursday: Late Night 10.00–20.00. Sunday: 11.00–17.00.   Entry Free.
Web: www.butlergallery.ie. Tel: 056-7761106.

Bowling

The K-Bowl, located at MacDonagh Shopping Centre provides 10-pin bowling with 10 lanes. In addition, it has hurricane karts, a cross between bumpers and a hovercraft, pool tables and arcade games. It may not be the restful place you hoped for but, on a wet day with noisy teenagers, it can be a godsend. The lanes are wheelchair accessible.
11am – 10pm seven days a week.. Tel: 056-7788200. Web: www.kbowlkk.ie.

Camp sites

Tree Grove caravanning and camping site is located on the R/00 Bennettsbridge Rd, 150m from the J5 junction. It has 30 pitches and is open from March to mid-November. It is within easy walking distance of the city centre. Tel: 056-7770302. www.kilkennycamping.com

Nore Valley Park is 3 km from Bennettsbridge, on the road to Stoneyford, turning right just before the bridge coming from the city Located deep in the countryside, it has 60 pitches, offers free showers and hot water. It also provides free access to the farm next door.
Open March - October. www.norevalleypark.com Tel: 056-7727229.

Canoeing and Kayaking

Discover the countryside from a different side. Travelling through the country by river makes the familiar look new. There are two operators who will float your boat, mainly on the River Barrow.

With Pure Adventure you can canoe or kayak on the Barrow, Nore or Suir rivers for half a day or all day. They also have SUP boarding (Stand Up Paddling) on the Barrow at Graiguenamanagh. Tel: 087-2265550. Web: www.pureadventure.ie

Go With The Flow River Adventures cater for groups and those who want to do their own thing. Suitable for families, they take children from 6 years of age upwards. "Discovery River Adventure" guided tours take part each weekend. They also provide 2 and 3-day packages, with B&Bs located along the route. Phone 087-2529700. Web: www.gowiththeflow.ie.

Children

While the delights of a medieval city are to some tastes, even the most patient of children will want something more. Kilkenny has something for the family in need of some fun and some down time.

1. The best place for young families is the Castle Park. With acres of open ground, it is a safe and busy place for children. At the side opposite the entrance from the main road is a path leading to a safe playground with swings and slides for younger children. Look for the map inside the gate.

If you continue along the right hand path past the playground, and take the next path to the left you pass the Butler family graves which has a grave to Sandy, a family pet, which is a constant source of wonder to small children.

Passing by and bearing to the right a woodland walk carries you down to the duck pond, which is a wild life sanctuary with a number of varieties of wild birds, including swans. Bring bread to feed them. Watch for squirrels who live in the trees as you walk along.

Be sure to bring a picnic as the grounds have a number of tables for outdoor dining, while the kids run free.

2. Climb St Canice's Tower. This may not be for the young members of the family but provides a thrill for teenagers, even those who are only so at heart. (page 51)

3. Visit St Victoria. There is a certain gruesome thrill from visiting St Mary's Cathedral to see the wax dummy encasing the saint's bones. (page 35)

4. For children who did not grow up in the country side, a visit to Kilkenny Mart can be a very exciting experience. Why not visit Kilkenny mart where the real business of farming is carried out? (page 139)

5. On a wet day, go bowling in the K-Bowl at MacDonagh Junction. (page 133)

6. Take a road train trip from Kilkenny Castle and see the city sites without battling along the footpaths. Trips last about 30 minutes. For the older kids, there is a novelty in taking a guided cycling tour of the city. Starts near the Castle.

7. Go swimming in the Watershed, (page 140) part of a public sports complex on the Ring Road to the south of the city. It has a 25m pool, pay-as-you go gym, sauna, steam room and jacuzzi.

8. Go to the cinema. (Facing page)

9. For younger children visit a pet farm and see small animals or a trip to Jurassic Newpark to see llamas and moving dinosaurs is a treat. (page 139). For older children go to the National Reptile Zoo and get close to the unusual and exotic animals. (page 142)

10. Got a car? Travel to the Castlecomer Discovery Park (page 103) and try the junior zipwire or visit the fairy village?

Cinema

IMC Kilkenny is a multi-plex cinema located off the Old Mart Rd. It is a 15 min walk from the city centre. There is plenty parking. Check www.imccinemas.ie to see what is on show.

Climbing

For those with a head for heights, the Ballykeefe Quarry provides a good introduction to rock climbing for the novice. while also having grades up to E3 for those who have more experience. The rock is limestone and the quarry has a variety of climbs with bolted routes, colourfully called Dented Ego, Push your Granny and the Bishop's Nose, amongst others. Climbs range from 6m for novices to 30m for the more experienced.

While it will not be an easy option for the casual visitor, it might be worth having a look for when you come back on your next visit.

The Quarry is located between Kilkenny and Kilmanagh on the R695 (on signpost) aka L26A, 7.5 miles (12 km) from Kilkenny, 5 miles (8 km) from Callan.

On the way from Kilkenny, you pass through the village of Ballycallan in which is located the shop and pub known as 'The Pound' to which climbers usually repair. The road sweeps around to the south side of the hill, covered by Ballykeefe Wood. The quarry is clearly visible from the road.

Crafts

If you don't feel like working up a sweat, Kilkenny still has plenty for you. Kilkenny is a centre for contemporary craft and design. Look for the Trailkilkenny brochure at any hotel or the Kilkenny Tourist Office. It has a map showing craft businesses across the county. However, if you don't have the time to visit all, there are a few which are in easy reach and are destinations worth visiting.

The Kilkenny Design Centre, opposite the gates to Kilkenny Castle and the National Craft Gallery in the stables behind are a good place to get a flavour of what is on offer. In addition the stables are also home to a number of smaller craft businesses which are open to visitors and provide an opportunity to see crafts people at work. You can see the workers make one-off pieces and they are very open to talk to you about their work or Kilkenny.

Outside the city, travel south 10km to Bennettsbridge. Just before the bridge turn right and travel along by the river a short distance to the large building on your left, which has ample parking. Formerly a grain mill, this is now the workshop of Nicholas Mosse, whose hand thrown pottery decorated with sponge work is exported around the world. A shop and café are on site.

Further south by another 10km, through Thomastown and past Jerpoint Abbey, is the sign post for Jerpoint Glass. Here for over 40 years, the Leadbetter family have been producing their own unique hand made glass. Not only is there a shop to buy the vases, bowls and stemware but, at certain times, there are demonstrations of the art of glassblowing. These are from 10am to 4pm Monday to Thursday and 10am to 1pm on Fridays. No demonstrations on Bank holidays.

Finally, the Craftyard at Castlecomer Demesne (page 103) provides a range of crafts businesses, from pottery to stonework. There is something for everyone here.

Cycling

Independent cycling around Kilkenny is being catered for with four marked tours around the county. Details of maps and routes are available on the Trail Kilkenny website.

The North Kilkenny Route takes in Tullaroan, Freshford, Ballyragget and Castlecomer and is approx 82km long and fully sign posted. The 64km long East Kilkenny Route travels through Thomastown, Graiguenamanagh and Gowran.

The shorter 41km South Kilkenny Loop winds through back roads past Bennettsbridge,

Stoneyford and Kells. A North Kilkenny Loop of 27km brings you to Jenkinstown Woods and Dunmore Caves.

For those who lack the stamina for such efforts, the Bike'n' Hike option from Kilkenny Cycling Tours is worth considering. The tour involves a quiet cycle of 10km on a quiet back road to Bennettsbridge, where you rest, followed by a riverside hike back to base. Web: www.kilkennycyclingtours.com. Tel: 086-895 4961

Distillery Tour

Ballykeefe Distillery Visitor Centre is open to those who want to know more about the history of Irish Whiskey and see whiskey, gin and poitin being distilled today on a working farm. It is just 15 minutes from the city but you will need a car to get there. Booking is necessary. Web: www.ballykeefedistillery.ie. Tel: 087-7004538

Festivals

Whenever you plan your trip, you are likely to arrive during one of Kilkenny's many festivals. In the in '60s, Kilkenny was famous for its Beer Festival. Now gone, it has been replaced by a selection to satisfy a wide range of tastes. The following is a list of some of the longer running ones. However, new ones seem to arrive every year.

1. Kilkenny Arts Festival. The daddy of them all. Held in August each year, it hosts the best in contemporary classical music and art, with a sprinkle of traditional and world music and a busy fringe scene. Check www.kilkennyarts.ie

2. Cat Laughs Festival. Going for over almost 30 years, this weekend long festival, held on the June Bank holiday weekend, showcases a range of comedians from home and abroad. Many big names stood up in front of a Kilkenny crowd before they became famous. www.thecatlaughs.com

3. Kilkenny Roots Festival. For those whose music is a little less manufactured and closer to its beginnings, with a leaning towards Americana, then the May Bank holiday weekend in Kilkenny is the place to be. www.kilkennyroots.com

4. Savour Kilkenny. The big food festival in the South East. Held every year on the October Bank Holiday weekend, the Parade plaza turns into a giant food fair and local restaurants put out their best menus. www.savourkilkenny.com

5. Kilkenomics. It shouldn't work but each year it proves it does. Europe's first economics festival that mixes the top economic minds with some of the country's brightest comedians, is suitably held in the dark November nights. If you want to laugh or cry, this is the place to be. www.kilkenomics.ie

Footgolf

A combination of golf and football, footgolf can be double the pleasure or double the frustration. With shorter holes, it is ideal for families and footballs can be rented. Pococke Footgolf is adjacent to junction 8 on the Ring Road.

Tel: 056-7775644 Email: pocockegolf@gmail.com.

Gardens & Parks

Not every out door activity needs to involve a sweating brow. County Kilkenny has a variety of gardens for those who take a gentler pleasure in what nature has to offer. Find details in this book for the Tudor garden at Rothe House (page 39), the arboretum and woodland walks of Woodstock (page 91), the rose garden and parkland of Kilkenny Castle (page 23), the hidden garden of Butler House (page 25), the fairy garden of Kilfane (page 90) and the ghostly garden of Shankill Castle (page 100).

Another interesting garden visit is the Watergarden in Ladywell, Thomastown. This is an initiative for people with special needs and incorporates a garden centre, art gallery and a formal water garden. The Watergarden is open Tuesdays to Fridays from 10am until 4pm. Closed Saturdays and Sundays.

Genealogy

If your family roots are in Kilkenny, then you may want to look up the records and find out about that black sheep. While much o the public records are being put online, they just give the basic details and require some level of patience and persistence to get the full story.

Rothe House is the genealogy centre for Kilkenny, with a computerised database. The genealogist can be contacted at kilkennyfamilyhistory@rothehouse.com. A 20-minute consultation can also be booked on Tuesday afternoons.

There is also a library of Kilkenny newspapers from the 18th century to date which can be accessed by appointment. Tel. 056 - 7722893.

Golf

Whether a good walk spoiled or the best way to get out and enjoy the great outdoors, Kilkenny has a variety of golf clubs. Most prominent is the Jack Nicklaus designed parkland course at Mount Juliet, which Tiger Woods described as having perfect fairways, when he played them.

Web: www.mountjuliet.ie Tel: 056-7773071   email golfreservations@mountjuliet.ie

Kilkenny GC. Glendine, Kilkenny. A par 71 championship course. Tel: 056-7765400 web: www.Kilkennygolfclub.com email: enquiries@kilkennygolfclub.com

Callan GC. 1 mile from Callan on the Knocktopher Road. Par 72 course with water features on 8 of the holes.

Web: www.callangolfclub.net Tel. 056-7725136 email: info@callangolfclub.net

Castlecomer GC. Set between a 200 year old forest and a river, this is a small but challenging course. Web: www.castlecomergolf.ie Tel: 056-4441139 email: info@castlecomergolf.ie

Gowran GC. A par 71 course set partly in the centre of Gowran Park racecourse.

Web: www.gowranpark.ie Tel: 056-7726699 email. golf@gowranpark.ie

Pococke Golf Course, Johnswell Road, Kilkenny. Just beside junction 8 on the Ring Road, this is a pay-as-you-go 18 hole par-three golf course with club hire, golf shop and shop for snacks and refreshments. Tel: 056-7755466.

In addition, there is an independent driving range in Kilkenny. Newpark Golf Driving Range is located off the Castlecomer Road. Take the road to the right directly across from the Broguemaker Pub and travel for 1km. The range is on your left. It has enclosed bays and plenty of outdoor grass space. Tel. 056-7752205.

Horse Racing

Gowran Park has Grade 1 status and has 16 top quality national hunt and flat meets each year. There is at least one meeting each month. There has been much investment in developing the course and facilities in the last few years and the course is on a par with the best in Ireland at this stage. You don't need to be a hardened racing enthusiast to enjoy a day in wooded countryside listening to the thunder of hooves and the shouts of an excited crowd. Watch the papers for a race. The course is beside Gowran village located on the R448 to Thomastown.

Web: www.gowranpark.ie. Tel: 056-7726225.

Horse Riding & Pony Trekking

The Moloney family at Warrington on the south of the city have generations of horsemanship in the blood. Warrington Top Flight is their large equestrian centre with an indoor jumping arena. In addition to lessons, they also have trekking along by the banks of the River Nore, which is beside the centre. This is suitable for experienced riders as well as novices and they can match a horse to your standard.

To get to the centre, travel 2.5km from the Castle out the R700 to Bennettsbridge. There is a large stone name marker for Top Flight on the left hand side. The centre is 1 km down this country lane. Tel: 056-7722682

Mount Juliet Equestrian Centre on the Mount Juliet Estate is home to the Ballylinch Stud. The Centre has indoor and outdoor jumping areas and the wide estate provides many trails for trekking, trail riding and cross country schooling for those who want to prepare for show jumping or hunting.

Tel: 056-7738562 email: info@mjequestrian.ie Web: www.mjequestrian.com

Hurling

Want to know more about hurling? Try the Kilkenny Way Hurling Experience in the city. A two hour crash course (and meal) in the science of the game. Not only do you get to hear about the game but you get to learn the basic skills at Nowlan Park, home of Kilkenny hurling.

Tours daily are at 2pm weekdays and 12am on weekends, from Lanigan's Bar in Rose Inn St, which has a great hurling themed bar room. Web: www.thekilkennyway.ie Tel: 0868171978.

For a different approach, which takes you out of the city, there are two options for you. Malzard's Pub and Hurling Experience is in Stoneyford, about 15km south of the city. It makes great use of the field at the back of the pub premises, with experienced hurlers to show you how to wield the mighty hurl. There is a little walking involved and the comfort and attraction of a family owned pub is only the puck of a ball away. The neighbourhood artisan cheese-maker is also on hand to provide diversion. Web: www.malzards.com   Tel: 087-9715304

In the north of the county, Hurling Tours Ireland use the village green in Freshford to bring out your inner Cuchullain. Back in Kavanagh's pub (an integral part of the tour) you learn how hurleys are made. Web: www.hurlingtoursireland.ie. Tel: 087-9700795.

For the real experience, watch a match. They are played regularly throughout the summer. Check for upcoming games on www.kilkennygaa.ie. Most games are in the towns and villages around the county and if you arrive, there will always be a local to show you where the local playing field is, unless you see a crowd of supporters already walking to the gate.

Karting

On the Waterford side of Ballyhale, about 25km from Kilkenny city, is Kiltorcan Raceway, a karting circuit. It has a 1 km smooth, all weather, floodlit track. Event races can be organised for groups of 10 or more people and short practice sessions can also be organised for smaller groups. Drivers from 10 years old upwards can take part.

As it is a popular event, you should phone ahead before calling out, to make sure you are not left waiting. www.kiltorcan.com or Tel: 087-2464872

Mart

Have you been raised in an urban environment and never seen where your food comes from? Visit Kilkenny Mart where the real business of farming is carried out. Located at Cillín Hill on the Carlow Road (R712), 1 km from Junction 6 on the Ring Rd, the mart has sheep sales at 10am on Monday morning followed by calf sales on Tuesday and cattle sales on Thursdays at 10am. There are other sales organised at irregular times during the week.

It is a chance to see big animals in large numbers in a busy environment. Something a town or city dweller rarely gets a chance to see. There's also a cafe on site.

Tel: 056-7721407 email: info@kilkennymart.ie

Museums

For those who crave a little history, there are a number of places which will give you what you want.

The daddy of all sites in the city is Kilkenny Castle, where the story of Kilkenny and the ruling Butler family is joined with the story of the building. (Page 18)

The main museum in town is the Medieval Mile Museum (See page 27) This tells the broad history of Kilkenny and has a unique collection of medieval and Renaissance-style tombs in the adjacent graveyard.

Rothe House (Page 39) is an original Elizabethan merchant's house. Although it is not extensively equipped as a museum, it has some interesting items on display and a restored medieval garden to enjoy.

The Smithwicks Experience across the road from it is a more modern presentation of the history of brewing in Kilkenny (Page 38).

St Canice's Cathedral also has its own take on Kilkenny's history with an obvious leaning towards the religious history. (Page 48)

Finally, the bizarre experience of a walk through a famine workhouse converted into a modern shopping centre while listening to the history of those who lived and died there makes for an unusual day shopping. Try the Famine Experience available at the customer service desk in MacDonagh Junction. It's free. (Page 62)

Pet Farms

For an authentic farm experience, visit Nore Valley Park Pet Farm. Travel south 10km to Bennettsbridge on the R700. Turn right before the bridge and take the road to road towards Stoneyford for 3km. In addition to the chance to cuddle a rabbit, or get close to chicks, lambs and ducks, there are also trailer rides, pedal go-karts, straw bouncing, crazy golf and a maze. With 3km of walks and a picnic area, there is plenty to tire out the busiest young visitor. What more could you want? Open Monday to Saturday 9am to 6pm. Closed Sundays.

Web: www.norevalleypark.com. Tel: 056-7727747.

For greater excitement, try Jurassic Newpark. Part of the Newpark Hotel on the Castlecomer Road. In addition to meeting sheep, donkeys, alpaca and llamas, you also get to meet twelve moving lifesize dinosaurs. Visitors welcome.

Web: www.jurassicnewpark.com. Tel: 056-7760500

Pitch and Putt

An Irish game, invented in Co Cork in the 1930's, pitch and putt is not a small relation to golf. Rather it has become a sport which needs a different set of skills and thought.

Also, unlike golf it is a more democratic game which the family can play together, (as long as you are over 10 years of age).

If you would like to try this game, the city Lacken pitch and putt course located on the grounds of St Canice's hospital on the Dublin Rd. It is open 7 days a week from 9:30am until dark. Tel: 086-8661105. Web: http://lackenpitchandputt.weebly.com

Pubs

You don't need a guidebook to find a pub in Kilkenny. However, there are a few worth having a look at. Tynans Bridge House bar at John's bridge has a traditional horse shoe bar and relics from when it also functioned as a grocery and a pharmacy. This is the real thing and always busy at night.

Langtons bar in John St is a busy place. There are multiple bars, a busy restaurant, a boutique hotel and a theatre. Langtons is the place where everyone meets everyone and can be very busy at weekends.

Kytelers Inn in Kieran St has a unique story. What's not to like about a pub which once housed a witch and her acolytes. During the high season it has Traditional Irish music nightly.

The Brewery Corner in Parliament St is the place to go and try the taste of a range of beers from Irish micro-breweries.

In 2016 Sullivan's Brewing Company resurrected itself. Closed since 1918, as the result of a duel over a lady, the 21st century descendant makes craft beer which is sold at Sullivan's Taproom in John St.

In addition to this selection, there is one to suit everyone. If you don't like where you are, drink up and try next door.

Running

Many of the roads around the city are country roads, which are narrow with blind bends and traffic. These are not safe for recreational running. The best place is the Castle Park which has a 2km circuit if you stick by the wall around the park. Each Saturday at 9:30am, the local Parkrun also meets here which gives you the opportunity of a competitive workout and a chance to cave a coffee and a bun later with some fellow runners.

River activities

If the canoeing and kyacking options don't float your boat, there are other choices if you just want to see the scenery. There are daily boat trips on the River Nore, starting near the castle. It is a chance to see some wild life as well as the city from a different angle.

Web: www.boattrips.ie. Tel: 087-2061999.

Shopping

Part of the fun in shopping is the search, so we are not going to list out all Kilkenny's shops for you. That would spoil the pleasure.

The city has two main shopping centres. MacDonagh Junction, at the end of John St farthest from the river, is home to a range of international and national outlets, from H&M to T K Maxx. Fashion chains River Island, Next, Pamela Scott and Jack & Jones are also there. The centre also has a courtyard surrounded by food outlets giving all your group a choice of what to eat. There is a large underground car park at the centre.

The main shopping area in the city is High St, which is a street of individual shop shapes, sizes and designs, reflecting the housing styles of the last few centuries. Many of the shops are locally owned, so you are likely to get a choice not available across the country. For clothes, the two largest are Pauls and Goods, two department stores which are across from each other near the Tholsel building. Further along the street is the entrance to Market Cross, an off street shopping centre, which is always busy.

Swimming

For those who like the rush of flowing water when they swim, the River Barrow in Graiguenamanagh is a popular swimming place. The best place is near the boat club where diving boards are a centre of attraction. There are life guards on duty during the summer.

Three miles north of the town is Clashganny lock which is also a popular spot and is also overseen by lifeguards in the summer.

For a more civilised and controlled location, the indoor swimming pool at the Watershed in Loughboy, Kilkenny provides for all the family. In addition, there is a pay-as-you-go gym, to get your fitness level on tune for your active holiday. Located at Junction 4 on the Ring Road to the south of the city, there is ample car parking.

Open: Mon - Fri: 7:30am - 10pm. Sat: 9am - 6pm. Sun & Bank Holidays: 10am - 6pm.

Web: www.thewatershed.ie Tel: 056-7734620

Taxis

There are four taxi ranks in the city. They are located at the Parade, beside the Left Bank, on Bateman quay, near the Lady Desart bridge, on John St, beside St John's church and at the railway station. There are many independent taxis. However , a few have multiple drivers, ensuring they have someone available all the time. The largest is Seven 7s at 056-7777777.

Also try Kilkenny Taxis at 056-7722224 or 087-2255333

Theatre:

The Watergate Theatre in Parliament St has a year round program of plays and concerts. With touring shows, local amateur productions, ballet, opera and musicals, you might just be in town when your favourite theatrical performance is on.

Web: www.watergatetheatre.ie Tel: 056-7761674 email: boxoffice@watergatetheatre.com

The Set Theatre in John St is located beside Langtons Hotel in John St. and part is of the same complex. It hosts a programme of mainly musical or comedy events.

web: www.set.ie email: set@langtons.ie

Cleere's Bar & Theatre at 28, Parliament St faces the Watergate Theatre. The theatre is located at the back of the premises and occasional performances of live bands and small production theatre. Web: www.cleeres.com Tel: 056-7762573

Tourist Information

The main Tourist Office is on High St. Close to the Tholsel. It is a good place to start by getting a map of the city.   Tel: 1800-230330

In addition, along High St are a number of guideposts with maps and some information on what is nearby.

Tours

The best way to see anywhere is in the company of someone who knows it intimately. Kilkenny is well supplied with options for all tastes. Almost all tours require pre-booking.

Kilkenny Walking Tours is the longest 'running' tour in the city. With years of experience, they know all there is to know. Over 90 minutes of gentle strolling, you get a good street level lesson in the city's past. Tours are at 11am and 2pm daily, Monday to Saturday, meeting in front of the Tourist Office. This is Ireland It can get wet. Dress appropriately.

Web: www.kilkennywalkingtours.ie. Tel: 087-2651745.

A notable alternative is the Ormonde Language Tour which, in addition to English, also provides tours in French and German.

Web: www.ormondelanguagetours.com. Tel: 087-6290244.

Kilkenny has two road train tours which start and finish at the Parade Tower of Kilkenny Castle. Both take in the same sights and have a recorded commentary of the sights and the buildings on route. They can be a welcome alternative if you are footsore, have young children, find the thought of a walk through busy streets too much work or are just plain lazy.

The trips take about 25 minutes and operate from mid-March to October.

Web: www.kilkennycitytours.com Tel: 086-7301500 or

Web: www.kilkennyroadtraintours.com. Tel: 087-6778832

For an alternative view, Kilkenny Cycling Tours operate guided tours of the city with a local guide. It speeds you past the bits you don't want to see and keeps you off the footpaths, which can get crowded and busy during the summer. Also, you get a gentle workout for the body and the mind at the same time.

Web: www.kilkennycyclingtours.com. Tel: 086-8954961

For a more personal tour, you can have your own chauffeur bring you on a tailored tour of the county. Web: www.kilkennytaxitours.com Tel: 086-8680166.

Finally for something different. An alternative view of Kilkenny is told in the Kilkenny Ghost Tour. Participants dress appropriately in witch's caps and pointed hats to protect them from the supernatural. Web: www.kilkennyghosttours.com Tel: 086-3570572.

For the real story try Kilkenny Haunted Dark Tours. Call Sharon at 087-623 0932.

Finally if you have had too many guided tours, you might try Shenanigans for a misguided tour of the city. Jokes magic and history shine a new light on Kilkenny's past. Web: www.shenaniganswalks.ie. Tel: 087-274 3865

Walking

For a wide selection of walking routes around the county, the Trail Kilkenny brochure, which is widely available, gives a generous choice. These are also accessible through apps for the iPhone or Android.

The walks go from the gentle, which are on level ground suitable for walking with a buggy, to more strenuous longer distance tramps such as the Nore Valley Walk, which currently runs from Kilkenny to Bennettsbridge but is being extended in time to continue the journey beside the River Nore.

In the city, the Castle park (see page 23) has a variety of experiences from formal walks to walking with wildlife along the woodland parts at the far end.

Another interesting walk in the city is along the river and canal. Starting at John's Bridge, there is a pathway along the river, beneath the walls of the Castle's grounds. This takes you by the river and after a short distance under tree shaded walks by a small old canal. The walk is paved and level the whole way and suitable for buggies. The first 1 km follows the wall of the Castle Park with a number of entrances into the grounds. Walking a further 1 km brings you to the end of the paved path. Along this path there is a new footbridge to bring you across the river and back to your start along the other side of the river. The hardy walker can continue along the river bank walk for a further two km, but it is a cross country walk, not suitable for everyone.

One walk in particular, which is something special for all the family, is through the woods at Jenkinstown Park, north of the city. The park is part of an old estate and the remnants of the Big House are still standing. Irish poet Thomas Moore wrote his immortal poem 'The Last Rose of Summer' while staying here.

The wood is small, only a few acres inside an old parkland wall, but it is filled with dark pine, giant beech and gnarled old oak & ash. In season, the ground can be covered with bluebells. There are two looped walks through the wood. The special attraction is an enclosed park with young deer which children can feed. A keen eye can spot squirrels and foxes in the wood. On a sunny day, bring a picnic.

To get there, take the road to Castlecomer. Five km after you pass the roundabout for the Ring Road around the city, turn left (fingerpost on opposite side of road). The park is 1.5km up this road. There is a junction half way up. Look out for the road sign.

Zoos:

The National Reptile Zoo is Ireland's only reptile zoo and a very unique experience. The purpose of the zoo is conservation and education and gives a very personal experience with reptiles. Not only do you see snakes, lizards, scorpions, crocodiles, alligators and frogs but, in the reptile handling zone, you get to handle and touch some of them. It is a big hit with children who get to see up close animals they would normally only see on TV. The zoo is located indoors in Hebron Industrial estate, which is a 10 minute walk from MacDonagh Shopping Centre. Web: www.nationalreptilezoo.ie Tel: 056-7761783.

Index

Page   Page

Index

If you have enjoyed this book and found it useful, then it has served its purpose. However, you may have found it contained errors or left something out, which you needed to know about. If so, please let us know at aboutkilkenny@outlook.com and we will try to fix it in future editions.